# LYSTRA

**3**

(3) *Founder of Colonia Lystra tracing limits of city with a plow drawn by a white bull and a cow*

**4**

(4) *Heracles of Derbe with a club. Coin of Antoninus Pius, A.D. 138–161.*

**7**

(7) *City goddess of Lystra, sitting on rocks, with crescent on her head and grain-ears in her hand. A river is at her feet*

**8**

(8) *Victory writing on a shield, probably from a statue at Derbe. Coin of Empress Lucilla*

W. M. Ramsay

# GUIDANCE FROM
# GALATIANS

# GUIDANCE FROM GALATIANS

## A New

- Commentary
- Workbook
- Teaching Manual

## DON EARL BOATMAN

President of Ozark Bible College
Joplin, Missouri

*Paraphrase* **by James MacKnight**

**College Press, Joplin, Missouri**

Copyright 1961
Don Earl Boatman

# DEDICATION

To my mother and father who gave to us children the priceless gift of a knowledge of God's Word, pure, simple, and without denominational names, creeds or customs.

With deep affection, I dedicate this book of my faith and conviction, to my parents, with the hope that I can give to others a portion of what these have given to me.

# Contents and Analytical Outline of the Epistle to the Galatians

## PART ONE — ANALYSIS

### PAUL'S DEFENSE OF HIS APOSTLESHIP AND THE GOSPEL 1:1 - 2:21

8

# PREFACE

The Book of Galatians is an inspiring book to read and to study. It is a doctrinal book with logic to challenge the thinking person, and with truth to edify those who are confused on the subject of the Christian's relationship to the old covenant.

I have not spent time on The North Galatian Theory. The truths of the book are applicable to all men. The works of the flesh are to be avoided by all men east, west, north and south while the fruits of the Spirit are to be enjoyed by men everywhere.

The notes of this book were first developed in my early years of teaching in Minnesota Bible College. I appreciate the inquiring minds who helped me to search for the profound truth of the Gospel.

Mrs. Donald Fream, Professor in Ozark Bible College, worked laboriously to make the manuscript worthy of a typist's labors. Mrs. Russell Watts, the wife of a minister, and mother of two small sons, worked sacrificially as the typist.

If this book is valuable, Don De Welt who urged and prodded me to write it should receive credit beyond the comprehension of all who have never published a book.

I pray earnestly that the readers may find this book to be practical, and that through the study of it they will come to a greater appreciation of the one great book which alone is inspired.

## GENERAL INTRODUCTION TO THE EPISTLE TO THE GALATIANS

I. TO WHOM WRITTEN. This is a unique epistle in that it is written to a group of churches. It is not to a single congregation, nor to a city people, but to the churches of a district: Galatia.

A. The Location.
  1. It was in central Asia Minor.
  2. The province was one part of the district

B. The History Before Paul.
  1. The Territory.
    a. It originally belonged to the Phrygians.
    b. Certain tribes of Gauls (French) in their restless conquest-loving spirit invaded the land. These tribes tried to overrun Greece, but were repulsed and settled in this area, which bore their name eventually.
  2. The Dates of Important Events.
    a. They originally settled about 279 B.C.
    b. In 189 B.C., they were conquered by the Romans, but allowed to keep their own king.
    c. In 25 B.C. their self-government was taken away.
  3. The Division of the Galatians.
    a. They were divided into three tribes, each occupying sub-districts.
    b. The cities of Tavium Persinus and Anarya (now Angora) were their capitols.

C. The People.
  1. The Race.
    a. The majority were of the Celtic race, ancestors of the modern French, Welsh, Irish, and Scotch.
    b. Phrygians, Greeks, Jews and Romans also settled there.
  2. Language.
    a. The main language was Greek, the universal language.
    b. They also retained the Gallic tongue until the fourth century, when, according to Jerome, they could converse with the French.

3. Character.
   a. Julius Caesar says, "The infirmity of the Gauls is that they are fickle in their resolves and fond of change, and not to be trusted."
   b. Thierry says, "Frank, impetuous, impressible, eminently intelligent, but at the same time extremely changeable, inconsistant, fond of show, perpetually quarreling, the fruit of excessive vanity."
   c. Paul says, "I marvel that ye are so quickly removing from him that called you in the grace of Christ unto a different gospel . . . O foolish Galatians, who did betwitch you, before whose eyes Jesus Christ was openly set forth crucified?" (Galatians 1:6, 3:1)

D. Paul's Experience With the Galatians.
   1. Paul and company set sail to Perga in Pamphylia. Acts 13:13
      a. Lycaonia, Pisidia, Phmphylia, and a large part of Phrygia were in Galatia.
      b. The letter here may have been to the northern Galatians.
      c. Probably Antioch, Iconium, Lystra and Derbe were the churches, for these were in Paul's journey on his first visit.
   2. Paul's visit among them is recorded in detail in Acts 14.
   3. His journey through Phrygia and Galatia is recounted in Acts 16:6 and 18:23.

II. THE PAULINE AUTHORSHIP.
   A. Stated. Galatians 1:1
   B. Indicated. Galatians 6:11

III. THE DATE.
   A. The dating is not scientifically accurate as yet.
   B. It was written after his visit of Acts 18:23, which occurred about 54 - 58 A.D.; therefore, 57 A.D. is about right.

IV. THE PLACE OF WRITING.
   A. Macedonia is a possibility.
   B. Corinth is a possibility.

## V. THE PURPOSE OF WRITING.

A. To Overcome the Influence of Judaising Teachers.

B. To Establish His Apostleship.

1. The Judaisers felt the necessity of destroying Paul's influence.

2. They sought to do this by denying that he was an apostle of Christ.

## VI. THE RELATION OF THE EPISTLES OF GALATIANS AND ROMANS.

A. The relation of the Law to the Gospel is discussed in both.

B. Justification by obedience to God by faith in Christ and not by works of the Law is discussed in both.

## Study Questions

1.  Why is this a unique epistle?

2.  Where was Galatia located?

3.  What was the nature of the people of Galatia?

4.  What was Paul's experience with them?

5.  Where in Acts do we read of Paul's preaching to them?

6.  Did Paul make an effort to prove that the epistle was from his hand?

7.  How many times did Paul visit them?

8.  Tell of the apparent purpose of this letter.

9.  How is Galatians related in subject matter to Romans?

PART ONE   —   ANALYSIS

## PAUL'S DEFENSE OF HIS APOSTLESHIP AND HIS GOSPEL
### 1:1-2:21

A. INTRODUCTION. 1:1-10

1. Personal Greting. 1:1-5

a) Source and Agency of his Apostleship. 1:1

b) His Association in the Gospel. 1:2

### Text 1:1,2

**1 Paul, an apostle (not from men, neither through man, but through Jesus Christ, and God the Father, who raised him from the dead), 2 and with all the brethren that are with me, unto the churches of Galatia:**

### Paraphrase

1 Paul an apostle, not sent forth from any society of men, neither appointed by any particular man, but by Jesus Christ, and by God the Father, who raised him from the dead, and after his resurrection sent him from heaven to make me an apostle;

2 And all the brethren who are with me, to the churches of Galatia. These brethren, by joining me in this letter, attest the truth of the matters I am going to relate.

### Comment 1:1

**an apostle**

1. Meaning—"One Sent Forth."

a. They were chosen by Christ and ordained by God.

b. They had power to work miracles.

c. They were inspired. Cf. John 16:13

2. Qualifications.

a. They were to be a witness of the resurrection. Acts 1:21,22

b. Their office ceased with their death.

3. Work.

a. Their work was pre-eminently that of founding churches.

b. They were sent to preach and make disciples.

**not from men, neither through man**

1. It was urged against Paul that he was just a messenger of other apostles.

2. Paul claimed he received his apostleship from the Lord. Cf. Acts 20:24; Galatians 1:12; 1:17; Acts 9:6; II Corinthians 11:5

**but through Jesus Christ**

1. It was from Jesus on the Damascus road; hence, there was no human mixture.
2. He was not to be known as a preacher from Tarsus but an apostle of Christ.

**and God the Father**

1. Requests are to be made of God for workers. Matthew 9:37,38
2. "And God hath set some in the church; first apostles, second prophets, thirdly teachers." I Corinthians 12:28

**who raised him from the dead**

1. The ability to raise the dead identifies the true God.
2. The God that would raise Jesus would sanction the calling of an apostle from heaven.
3. The Resurrection won victory over law, sin, flesh, world, devil, death, and hell.
4. Paul does not say "the God who created heaven and earth," but "God who raised Jesus"—this is His most important work.

## Comment 1:2

**all the brethren**

1. A probable list would include Titus, Timothy, Silas, and Luke.
2. "And there accompanied him as far as Asia, Sopater of Berœa, the son of Pyrrhus; and of the Thessalonians, Aristarchus and Secundus; and Gaius of Derbe, and Timothy; and of Asia, Tychicus and Trophimus." Acts 20:4 See also Acts 21:16.
 a. In these days we can hardly afford to have even one evangelist for more than two weeks.
 b. Paul took crews with him and stayed until the work was established.
 c. Today, evangelism is done on the basis of "How long can we, the church, stand his preaching and what can we afford?"
3. "The brethren" are not named probably because the Galatians were familiar with Paul's co-workers, either through personal visits or through correspondence.

**unto the churches of Galatia**

1. Some things are conspicuous by their absence.
 a. No single word of praise.
 b. No commendation.
2. This is unlike the Roman epistle.

16

## Study Questions 1:1,2

10. What did Paul claim for himself?
11. Define the term "apostle."
12. Was Paul's call a divine one?
13. Was Paul merely a preacher from Tarsus?
14. Tell who sent Paul.
15. Tell what God did to Christ to establish His authority to send apostles.
16. Find other scriptures that tell of the Apostle's call.
17. Give a probable list of brethren with Paul when he greeted the Galatians in the letter.
18. How does this compare in size to our modern day evangelistic teams?
19. How does his salutation differ from other greetings in other epistles?

c) Salutation 1:3-5

## Text 1:3-5

**3 Grace to you and peace from God the Father, and our Lord Jesus Christ, 4 who gave himself for our sins, that he might deliver us out of this present evil world, according to the will of our God and Father: 5 to whom be the glory for ever and ever. Amen.**

## Paraphrase

3 We wish grace to you, and happiness from God the Father, and from our Lord Jesus Christ, by whom the Father dispenses his blessings to men,

4 Because he gave himself to death for our sins, that he might deliver us from the bad principles, and practices, and punishment of this present evil age, agreeably to the will of our God and Father, who determined to save us by the death of his son.

5 To whom, for that unspeakable favour, be ascribed by angels and men, honour and praise, through all eternity. Amen.

## Comment 1:3

**Grace to you**
1. "Favor to you" is a single greeting stating that he was writing a friendly letter.
2. The grace is from God, or else Paul, a Jew, would not have had favor toward these indifferent Gentiles.

**peace from God**
1. *Salaam* (peace) is a typical oriental greeting, even today.

17

2. Real peace comes only through God and Christ.
a. "For he is our peace . . ." Eph. 2:14
b. "And he came and preached peace to you that were afar off, and peace to them that were nigh." Eph. 2:17
3. This peace is not from the Emperor, or from kings, or from governors, but from God the Father.
4. Peace differs from grace in that:
a. Grace remits sin; peace quiets the conscience.
b. Grace involves remission; peace makes a happy conscience.
c. Grace is God's favor; peace dispels fear.

**and from our Lord Jesus Christ**

1. One can not be of Jewish faith and have the favor of God and Christ.
2. The grace and peace of Christ is in the picture.

## Comment 1:4

**who gave himself for our sins**

1. He gave:
a. Not gold, not a paschal lamb, not an angel, but self.
b. Not a moral code, nor a new political scheme, but self.
2. He could have sent twelve legions of angels. Matt. 26:53
3. He gave himself humbly. Phil. 2:5-8
4. He gave Himself by the laws of Sacrifice, Ransom, and Justice.
5. Note the temptations; observe Gethsemane.

**for our sins**

1. He did not give Himself for a crown, a kingdom, or our goodness, but for our sins.
2. Sin is not maladjustment, but terrible transgression.
it means "missing the mark."
a. They are not small and insignificant, but mountainous.
b. We are not good moral men but sinners.
c. *Hermatia*, one of the Greek words for sins, catches all of us:

**that he might deliver us**

1. Man is lost; he does need saving; he does need help from God.
a. He is a slave.
b. He is a captive.
2. Too many people are not interested in salvation's delivery because they do not feel there is anything to be delivered from, but there is.

a. "Creatures without reason . . . to be taken and destroyed."
2 Pet. 2:12
b. "elements shall be dissolved . . ." 2 Pet. 3:8-11
c. ". . . they were judged every man according to their works."
Rev. 20:13
". . . this is the second death, even the lake of fire." v.14
". . . and if any was not found written in the book of life, he
was cast into the lake of fire." v. 15
d. John 3:14,15,16
e. ". . . the wrath of God . . ." Rom. 5:9
f. ". . . who delivered us from the wrath to come." I Thess. 1:10

### from this present evil world

1. Even our nation, so called Christian America, is evil.
a. Hear the curses on the night air.
b. Listen to the vileness in the shop.
c. Check the lists of roberries, murders, and adulteries.
d. Watch the gambling.
e. Look at the abused little children.
2. This evil world will be destroyed and a new heaven and a
new earth created. 2 Pet. 3:8-13; Rev. 21:1

### according to the will of God

1. Note these scriptures:
a. I John 4:10 "Herein is love, not that we loved God, but that
He loved us, and sent his Son to be the propitiation for our
sins."
b. Phil. 2:5-11 indicates the will of Christ.
c. Gethsemane indicates the will of Christ.
2. The will of God is responsible for salvation for the righteous
and punishment for the wicked.

### our God and Father

1. The Fatherhood of God is for both Christ and man.
a. Christ said to Mary Magdalene, "Go to my brethren, and say
unto them, I ascend unto my Father, and your Father; and
unto my God and your God." John 20:17
b. "Pray ye our Father," and the Lord's words in Matt. 6:9.
1) A Father loves
2) A Father provides
3) A Father protects
4) A Father gives
2. The will of God and Christ's will are in accord.

## Comment 1:5

**to whom be the glory for ever and ever. Amen.**

1. God is to have all and Paul none, even though he has argued for his apostleship.

2. Glory means praise, honor, renown, distinction, brilliance and splendor.

3. If we fail to direct glory to God now, we will not have an opportunity to glorify Him in heaven.

**Glory to God** — (Special exegetical outline)

1. Because it is commanded.

a. "Ascribe unto Jehovah, ye kindreds of the people, ascribe unto Jehovah glory and strength." I Chron. 16:28.

b. "Ye that fear Jehovah, praise him, all ye the seed of Jacob, glorify him; and stand in awe of him, all ye the seed of Israel." Psalm 22:23.

c. "Let them give glory unto Jehovah, and declare his praise in the islands." Isaiah 42:12

2. Because it is due Him. I Chron. 16:29; I Cor. 6:20

3. Because of His holiness. "Exalt ye Jehovah our God, and worship at his holy hill; For Jehovah our God is holy." Ps. 99:9
"Who shall not fear, O Lord, and glorify thy name? for thou only art holy; for all the nations shall come and worship before thee; for thy righteous acts have been made manifest." Rev. 15:4

4. Because of His mercy and truth.

a. "Not unto us, O Jehovah, not unto us, but unto thy name give glory for thy loving-kindness, and for thy truth's sake." Ps. 115:1

b. "And that the Gentiles might glorify God for his mercy." Rom. 15:9

5. Because of His faithfulness and truth.

a. "O Jehovah, thou art my God; I will exhalt thee, I will praise thy name; for thou hast done wonderful things, even counsels of old in faithfulness and truth." Isaiah 25:1

6. Because of His wondrous works.

a. "Insomuch that the multitude wondered, when they saw the dumb speaking, the maimed whole, and the lame walking,

and the blind seeing:  and they glorified the God of Israel."
Matt. 15:31

b. "For all men glorified God for that which was done." Acts 4:21

7. Because of His judgments.

a. "Therefore shall a strong people glorify thee, a city of terrible
nations shall fear thee." Isaiah 25:3

b. "I will be glorified in the midst of thee; and they shall know
that I am Jehovah, when I shall have executed judgments in
her." Ezekiel 28:22

c. "Fear God, and give him glory;  for the hour of his judgment
is come . . ." Rev. 14:7

8. Because of His deliverance.  Psalms 50:15

9. Because of His grace to others.

a. "And when they heard these things, they held their peace, and
glorified God, saying, Then to the Gentiles also hath God
granted repentance unto life." Acts 11:18

b. ". . . they glorify God . . . for the liberality of your contribution
unto them and unto all." 2 Cor. 9:13

c. ". . . and they glorified God in me." Gal. 1:24

## Study Questions 1:3-5

20. Does the word "grace" indicate "friendliness"?

21. What is the source of peace?

22. Would Paul have been so friendly to the Gauls if he were
not of God?

23. Discuss what peace from God does for people who love
barriers?

24. What does God's peace dispel in the human heart?

25. Name the two sources of peace found in this verse.

26. The word "who" refers to whom?

27. Why did Jesus give Himself?

28. How does His sacrifice compare with Old Testament sacrifices?

29. Is it fair to assume that sin is horrible, if Jesus died for our
sins?

30. Did Jesus give Himself, or did men kill Him?

31. Are all men sinners, or did He die for certain vile people?

32. Discuss the deliverance stated in verse four.

33. Why do we need it?

34. From what are we delivered?
35. What kind of punishment does the Christian escape?
36. What evidence do we have that our present generation is evil?
37. If we escape the punishment, what reward do we have in its place?
38. Whose will makes it possible?
39. Is divine will all that is necessary for salvation?
40. Define "glory."
41. Who is to be glorified?
42. How long does the glory last?
43. Why does God deserve glory? Name the reasons.

2. Occasion of the Epistle. 1:6-10
a) Their removal unto a different gospel. 1:6,7

## Text 1:6,7

**6 I marvel that ye are so quickly removing from him that called you in the grace of Christ unto a different gospel; 7 which is not another gospel: only there are some that trouble you, and would pervert the gospel of Christ.**

## Paraphrase

6 I wonder that ye are so soon removed from me, who called you into the gospel of Christ, which promises to sinners justification through faith; and that ye have embraced another gospel, or pretended message from God, concerning your justification;

7 Which is not another gospel, or message from God: But some there are, who, on pretence that their doctrine of justification by the law of Moses is authorized by God, trouble you with doubts concerning my doctrine, and wish to pervert the gospel of Christ.

## Comment 1:6

**I marvel**
1. This is not awful condemnation, but surprise.
2. This is a severe blow to one who believes as Paul expressed it in Romans 8:35-38—"Who shall separate us from the love of Christ?"
3. This is astonishing to one who believes in the Power of the Gospel and who has confidence in stability of man.

**so quickly removing**
1. Paul's labors to train a church are being overthrown in a short while.

2. Christianity is to be a thing of permanence, not a mushroom affair.
3. This is the opposite of what is required for salvation.
a. "Be thou faithful unto death." Rev. 2:10
b. "If we hold fast the beginning of our confidence firm unto the end." Heb. 3:14

### from him that called you

1. They had changed their spiritual location by turning to another gospel.
2. When men accept falsehood, they remove themselves from God.
3. The calling is expressed in I Thess. 2:12; 5:24; 2 Tim. 1:9.
4. Some insist that Paul is the one who called them, but Paul didn't say they were removed from him, but from Christ.

### in the grace of Christ

1. Truth had placed them in favor; now false teaching had made them unfavorable.
2. This knocks the idea that "sincerity alone is sufficient."
3. They were removed from grace: he does not say "peace."
4. God surely does not save them if they are removed from His favor.

### unto a different gospel

1. This "gospel" was Judaism mixed with Christianity.
a. The Jew insisted on Jewish ceremonies for Gentiles.
b. Paul establishes in this book that Judaism is not ever essential for Christians.
2. Think how awful then is Catholicism mixed with paganism and Judaism.
3. Protestantism, which is a mixture of paganism, Judaism, Catholicism, and Christianity, is likewise a different "gospel."

### Comment 1:7

### which is not another gospel

1. There are not two gospels to choose from, for "oneness" is characteristic of God.
a. "I am the truth." John 14:6
b. "There is one body, and one Spirit, even as also ye were called in one hope of your calling; one Lord, one faith, one baptism, one God and Father of all, who is over all, and through all, and in all." Ephesians 4:4-6
c. "But I fear, lest by any means, as the serpent beguiled Eve in his craftiness, your minds should be corrupted from the sim-

plicity and the purity that is toward Christ. For if he that cometh preacheth another Jesus, whom we did not preach, or if ye receive a different spirit, which ye did not receive, or a different gospel, which ye did not accept, ye do well to bear with him." 2 Cor. 11:3

2. These denominational folk who say "it doesn't make any difference" are either lying or they are terribly ignorant.

a. If it doesn't matter, why do they not preach the message that will produce unity?

b. It does make a difference to the preachers:

1) Their pension is at stake.

2) Their job is at stake.

3) Their denominational reputation is at stake.

c. It makes a difference to God. Cf. Gal. 1:8,9

### only there are some that trouble you

1. Urging circumcision and keeping of the law was a troublesome doctrine.

2. Denominationalists are trouble makers in binding commandments of men.

### and would pervert the gospel of Christ

1. Division is the beguiling of Satan, drawing men away from the simplicity of the gospel.

2. A creed is a perversion.

a. If it is like the Bible we do not need it.

b. If it is unlike the Bible, it is erroneous.

3. Infant baptism is an unscriptural doctrine, originated by an unscriptural church, practiced by unscriptural churches upon unscriptural candidates to save those unscriptural candidates from unscriptural sin.

## Study Questions 1:6,7

44. What surprised Paul?

45. Does this mean that the gospel lacks power?

46. Define "quickly removing."

47. Is this characteristic of good Christians?

48. Were they called?

49. Who did it and by what method?

50. What were they removed from?

51. Is this falling from grace?

52. Can you be in God's Church and participate in false teaching at the same time?
53. How different was the "different gospel"?
54. Harmonize Paul's expression "different gospel" and "not another gospel."
55. Is corrupted truth to be considered truth?
56. Is denominationalism wrong in the light of the Word of God?
57. Are false teachers, party teachers, etc., to be considered troublemakers to God?
58. If false teaching is troublesome, ought we to say that it doesn't make any difference what you believe as long as you are sincere?

b) Pronouncement of Divine Judgment upon Perverters of the Gospel.  1:8,9

## Text 1:8,9

**8 But though we, or an angel from heaven, should preach unto you any gospel other than that which we preached unto you, let him be anathema. 9 As we have said before, so say I now again, If any man preacheth unto you any gospel other than that which ye received, let him be anathema.**

## Paraphrase

8 They affirm that Peter preacheth, nay, that I myself preach justification by works of law. But even if we who write this, or an angel pretending to have come from heaven, should preach to you a method of justification contrary to, or different from, what we have formerly preached to you, let him be devoted to destruction.

9 To shew you how certain I am of the truth of the doctrine which I preach;  As we who write this letter said before jointly, so now a second time I separately say, if any man or angel preach to you concerning your justification, contrary to what ye have learned from me, let him be devoted to destruction.

## Comment 1:8,9

**but though we, or an angel from heaven**

1. Paul's fervency leads him to say that he, brethren, or angels of heaven should be accursed if they came with a perverted gospel.
2. The "we" probably means Paul specifically, but could include

all his preaching brethren.

### should preach unto you any gospel other

1. There is only one gospel, so there is no other gospel for us to hear.
2. Let us have faith in the gospel "once and for all delivered unto the saints." Jude vs.3

### than that which we preached unto you

1. Paul preached:
a. The death, burial and resurrection of Jesus. I Cor. 15:1-5
b. Belief in, and confession of, the Christ. Romans 10:9-10
c. Repentance from sin. Acts 17:30-31
d. Burial of sin repented-from. Romans 6:4
e. Resurrection from water to live in a new life. Romans 6:5

2. All gospel must be measured by this divine measure.

### let him be anathema

1. Let us examine the meaning of the word in the original language.
a. The Greek word *anathema* and the Hebrew *herem* mean "to accurse," "to damn."
b. "Let him be anathema" does not mean we are to curse him.

2. Many scriptures show the awfulness of false teaching.
a. "For there are many unruly men, vain talkers and deceivers, specially they of the circumcision, whose mouths must be stopped; men who overthrow whole houses, teaching things which they ought not, for filthy lucre's sake." Titus 1:10,11
b. "Now I beseech you, brethren, mark them that are causing divisions and occasions of stumbling, contrary to the doctrine which ye learned: and turn away from them." Romans 16:17
c. If any one cometh unto you, and bringeth not this teaching, receive him not into your house, and give him no greeting." 2 John 10
d. "Many will say to me in that day, Lord, Lord, did we not . . . by thy name do many mighty works?" Matt. 7:22
e. The Word of God is not to be added to, nor subtracted from. Rev. 22:18,19

3. In later years *anathema* came to mean excommunication (by the very ones who should have been accursed).
a. Excommunication meant separation from the church.

b. This is more than that, for angels were not in the church for man to excommunicate.

4. Verse nine differs only in the fact that Paul says that they received a gospel and therefore should not receive another one.

## Study Questions 1:8,9

59. What does the word "anathema" mean?
60. Who is included in the anathema?
61 Do we have modern day religions claiming to be from angels?
62. Name other verses that condemn false teachers.
63. How does verse nine differ from verse eight?
64. What may we assume by the emphasis of verse nine to verse eight?

c) His passion to please God. 1:10

## Text 1:10

**10 For am I now seeking the favor of men, or of God? or am I striving to please men? if I were still pleasing men, I should not be a servant of Christ.**

## Paraphrase

10 Having twice denounced destruction to myself and to all others, if we preach contrary to what was first preached to you, I now ask those who say I suit my doctrine to the humours of men, Do I by this denunciation make men my friends, or God? Or do I seek to please men? If indeed I still pleased men, as before my conversion, I should not be the servant of Christ.

## Comment 1:10

**seeking the favor of men**

1. He was not a time-serving, man-pleasing factionist, and such a condemnation was most unfounded.
a. His former life as a Pharisee — pleasing the priest or the people — directly in contrast to his suffering for the gospel.
b. In this connection, read 2 Cor. 6:4-10.
2. He would not be a servant of Christ if he were in the business of pleasing men.
a. On occasions however, he had conformed to men's customs.
1) He had Timothy circumcised. Acts 16:1-3
2) Paul and four others purified themselves at the temple. Acts 21:26
3) Paul shaved his head when he was at Cenchrea. Acts 18:18
b. These were done because of Paul's charitable disposition, but he never let down on doctrine.

B. PAUL'S GOSPEL AND APOSTLESHIP DIVINELY DE-
RIVED.  1:11-24
1. The divine source of his gospel.  1:11,12

## Text 1:11,12

**11 For I make known to you, brethren, as touching the gospel which was preached by me, that it is not after man. 12 For neither did I receive it from man, nor was I taught it, but it came to me through revelation of Jesus Christ.**

## Paraphrase

11 Now, because my doctrine hath been disregarded, on pretence that I was taught it by men, I assure you, brethren, concerning justification by faith, which was preached by me, that it is not a doctrine which I was taught by man, and which I was in danger of mistaking.

12 For I neither received it from Ananias, nor from any of the apostles at Jerusalem, nor was I taught it any how, except by a revelation from Jesus Christ.

## Comment 1:11

**not after man**

1. All instruction he received from men was for his own salvation.
a. "Rise and enter into the city, and it shall be told thee what thou must do." Acts 9:6
2. As God used human instrumentality for a divine message, so Paul had a divine message for men, but not from men.

## Comment 1:12

**nor was I taught it**

1. He didn't have any entrance or final examinations from men.
2. It was not received from the mouths or books of men.

**it came to me through revelation of Jesus Christ**

1. Just when Paul received this revelation is uncertain.
a. It could have been on the road to Damascus, for he started preaching at once — "straightway." Acts 9:20
b. Perhaps it was during his sojourn in Arabia. Gal. 1:17
c. It might have been each time he needed it, for Jesus had promised revelation to His apostles.
1) "He shall guide you into all truth." John 16:13
2) "The Holy Spirit shall teach you in that very hour." Luke 12:12
3) "For no prophesy ever came by the will of man: but men

spake from God being moved by the Holy Spirit." 2 Pet. 1:21
2. The subject matter of his revelation Paul makes clear to us.

## Study Questions 1:10-12

65. Whose favor did Paul seek?
66. Whose favor does the false teacher seek?
67. Why do men teach false doctrine according to Titus 1:11?
68. Give the source for Paul's message.
69. Why did Paul need to emphasize this?
70. Do people doubt his inspiration today?
71. Have you evidence that men denounce the apostles in their writing today?
72. How did Paul get his message?
73. When did it come to him?
74. Did it need to come all at once?
75. Were the other apostles taught all the truth at one time by Jesus?

2. Proof of its divine origin. 1:13-24
a) His early life was adverse to the gospel. 1:13,14

## Text 1:13,14

**13 For ye have heard of my manner of life in time past in the Jews' religion, how that beyond measure I persecuted the church of God, and made havoc of it: 14 and I advanced in the Jews' religion beyond many of mine own age among my countrymen, being more exceedingly zealous for the traditions of my fathers.**

## Paraphrase

13 To convince you of this, I appeal to my behaviour, both before and after I was made an apostle. Ye have heard, certainly, in what manner I behaved formerly, while I professed Judaism; that I exceedingly persecuted the church of God, and laid it waste.
14 And my enmity to the gospel was occasioned by my making progress in Judaism, (Acts 22:3), above many who were of the same age with myself in mine own nation; being more exceedingly zealous than any of them in maintaining the traditions of my fathers, in which, as a Pharisee, I placed the whole of religion.

## Comment 1:13

**beyond measure**
1. It was not a limited persecution—he went all out .
2. This zeal against the church spread his reputation as a persecutor.

### my manner of life in time past

1. He was of the strictest sect of the Pharisees. Phil. 3:5
2. He was zealous for the law, as were all good Pharisees.

### I persecuted the church

1. Paul consented to Stephen's death. Acts 8:1
2. "Because I persecuted the church of God." I Cor. 15:9
3. "I was before a blasphemer and a persecutor, and injurious." I Tim. 1:13
4. ". . . letters to bring them unto Jerusalem in bonds to be punished." Acts 22:4,5

### the church of God

1. Several names of the church are revealed in scripture.
a. The Church — Universal. Acts 9:31
b. Church of God — Planner. I Cor. 1:2
c. Church of the first born — Honor. Heb. 12:23
d. Body of Christ — Activity. I Cor. 12:27
e. Churches of Christ — Ownership. Rom. 16:16
f. Churches of saints — Character. I Cor. 14:33
g. Churches of the gentiles. Romans 16:4
2. Observe the significance of church names today.
a. They honor men.
b. They honor doctrines.
c. They honor forms of church government.

### made havoc of it

1. This, of course, refers to the people and not the buildings.
2. This was a strike against the authority of Christ.
a. "Gave him to be head over all things to the church." Eph. 1:22,23
b. "All authority hath been given unto me." Matt. 28:18
c. "Why persecutest thou me?" Acts 9:4

## Comment 1:14

### advanced in the Jews' religion

1. Was Paul the rich young ruler?
2. There are some who feel that he was.
a. Paul was called and was kicking against the goad. Acts 26:14
b. There is a possibility that this began when he went sorrowing away from Christ.
3. Hear what he says about himself:

a. "I also am an Israelite, of the seed of Abraham, of the tribe of Benjamin." Rom. 11:1

b. "If any other man thinketh to have confidence in the flesh, I yet more: circumcised the eighth day, of the stock of Israel, of the tribe of Benjamin, a Hebrew of Hebrews; as touching the law, a Pharisee; as touching zeal, persecuting the church; as touching the righteousness which is in the law, found blameless." Phil. 3:4-6

**being more exceedingly zealous**

1. Who else would travel like Paul to stamp out heresy as he was doing to the church?
2. Zeal characterized Paul, out of the church and in it, against it and for it.

**for the traditions**

1. What does tradition mean?
a. It can mean doctrine of God—"hold fast the traditions" (I Cor. 11:2).
b. It may mean doctrines of men as well as doctrines of the law here.
2. What were some traditions of men?
a. Jesus condemned the scribes and Pharisees for enlarging the borders of their garments.
b. The scribes and Pharisees held to wrong Sabbath observances, and condemned Christ for:
1) Healing. Matt. 5:1-10
2) Casting out demons. Luke 13:10-16
3) Plucking ears of grain. Matt. 12:1-8

**my fathers**

1. This may mean the patriarchs—Abraham, Isaac, Jacob, Moses, etc.
2. It may mean his own immediate religious fathers.
a. Perhaps Gamaliel, Paul's highly respected teacher, is meant. "There stood up one in the council a Pharisee, named Gamaliel, a doctor of the law, had in honor of all the people . . ." Acts 5:34 "I am a Jew . . . brought up in this city, at the feet of Gamaliel, instructed according to the strict manner of the law." Acts 22:3
b. Paul had a respect for his teachers, even though they were wrong.

## Study Questions 1:13,14

76. What is meant by "beyond measure"?
77. Tell of Paul's past.
78. Was he a trouble maker then?
79. What did he persecute?
80. What names does he give to the church?
81. Is there a name or are there names for the church?
82. Why are there scriptural names for the church?
83. Do we need to give new names to God's church?
84. How did Paul make havoc?
85. Discuss Paul's advancement.
86. How did he compare to others in zeal?
87. What does the word "tradition" mean?
88. Is it always a bad word when used religiously?
89. Name some traditions condemned by Jesus.
90. Do we have false teachers teaching them today?
91. Is a false teaching less evil when accepted by a respected denomination?
92. What does he mean by "fathers"?

b) His separation, call and early preaching were not from men. 1:15-17

## Text 1:15-17

**15 But when it was the good pleasure of God, who separated me, even from my mother's womb, and called me through his grace, 16 to reveal his Son in me, that I might preach him among the Gentiles; straightway I confered not with flesh and blood: 17 neither went I up to Jerusalem to them that were apostles before me: but I went away into Arabia; and again I returned unto Damascus.**

## Paraphrase

15 But when God, who destined me from my birth to be an apostle, and ordered my education with a view to that office, and who called me to it by his unmerited goodness, was pleased

16 To shew his Son to me, that I might preach Him to the heathen as risen from the dead, immediately after that I did not consult any man in Damascus, as having doubts concerning what I had seen, or as needing information concerning the gospel which I was called to preach.

17 Neither did I go up to Jerusalem to be instructed by they who were apostles before me; but I went away into Arabia, where there was no apostle; and having there received further revelations from Christ, and studied the scriptures by the light of these reevlations, I again returned to Damascus, without having seen any of the apostles.

## Comment 1:15

### when it was the good pleasure of God

1. God works on time. Cf. Gal. 4:4
2. He finds pleasure in His work and will.
a. "It was God's good pleasure through the foolishness of the preaching to have them that believe." I Cor. 1:21
b. "It is your Father's good pleasure to give you the kingdom." Luke 12:32

### who separated me

1. "Separate" is a Hebrew expression meaning to sanctify, ordain, or prepare.
2. Nothing Paul had done merited this call.
a. He was called from birth before he could do good.
b. He was called in sin while persecuting the church.
3. God had separated Paul—his call was not of man.
a. "Separated unto the gospel." Romans 1:1
b. "Separate me Barnabas and Saul." Acts 13:2
c. "Called to be an apostle." I Cor. 1:1

### even from my mother's womb

1. Paul could not know this except by inspiration.
2. Such separation was not unknown.
a. Moses — divine providence seen.
b. Samuel — God answered Hannah's request. I Sam. 1:1-20
c. John the Baptist — prophecy spoke of his coming. Lk. 1:5-25
d. Isaiah — "Listen O isles, unto me; and hearken, ye people, from far: Jehovah hath called me from the womb; from the bowels of my mother hath he made mention of my name." Is. 49:1
e. Jeremiah — "Before I formed thee in the belly I knew thee, and before thou camest forth out of the womb I sanctified thee; I have appointed thee a prophet unto the nations." Jer. 1:5

**and called me**
1. How many times was he called before he answered?
a. Many people waste many years rejecting the call.
b. Paul acted as though he were trying to make up for lost time.
2. Paul says, "I was not disobedient unto the heavenly vision."
   Acts 26:19

**through his grace**
1. Paul's wickedness was enough to bring wrath, but God's grace prevailed.
2. Grace called Paul to be an apostle, and grace gives us all an opportunity for salvation.

## Comment 1:16

**to reveal his Son in me**
1. The law pointed out sin— the gospel announces Christ is come.
2. Christ was revealed in Paul.
a. Paul was a good revelation of Jesus, for he was so consecrated.
b. Paul revealed Christ in a wide area, from Antioch to Rome, and (one theory says) even to Spain and Britain.

**that I might preach him among the Gentiles**
1. Paul states that his mission was to the Gentiles.
2. "But the Lord said unto him, Go thy way: for he is a chosen vessel unto me, to bear my name before the Gentiles and kings, and the children of Israel." Acts 9:15
3. Paul anounced to them a Saviour, not a lawgiver.
a. Paul is saying, "Do not listen to teachers of the law."
b. Listen not to the law, but to the gospel.
c. Listen not to Moses, but to the Son of God.

**straightway I conferred not with flesh and blood**
1. If God called and God revealed, then Paul didn't need any conference with men.
2. The disciples received their gospel from Christ, and so did Paul.

## Comment 1:17

**neither went I up to them that were apostles**
1. Evidently the apostles were staying close to Jerusalem.
2. Paul did not go up there to receive a message.

**I went away into Arabia**
1. The account in Acts 9 does not give any hint of Arabia.
2. He probably did not go to preach there.
a. "I . . . declared both to them of Damascus first, and at Jerusalem, and throughout all the country of Judea . . ." Acts 26:19,20

34

3. He does not say that he went there to receive a gospel, but he does say that he did not get it at Jerusalem.

**again I returned unto Damascus**

1. Here his first recorded ministry took place.

a. "And he was certain days with the disciples that were at Damascus." Acts 9:19

b. "And straightway in the synagogues he proclaimed Jesus, that he is the Son of God." Acts 9:20

c. "And when many days were fulfilled, the Jews took counsel together to kill him: . . . but his disciples took him by night, and let him down through the wall, lowering him in a basket." Acts 9:23

d. Perhaps after this he went to Arabia and then returned to Damascus (which is not mentioned in Acts 9), then he proceeded to Jerusalem. "And when he was come to Jerusalem, he assayed to join himself to the disciples: and they were all afraid." Acts 9:26

## Study Questions 1:15-17

93. How did God's good pleasure act in Paul?
94. When was God at work?
95. Why did Paul not heed the call?
96. When is the word "separation" used in Acts in relationship to Paul?
97. How did Paul know that God called him at birth?
98. Is this the first time God did this to men?
99. What was at work to give Paul a chance to answer the call?
100. How did Paul reveal Christ?
101. Name the places where Paul revealed the Lord.
102. Name the Gentiles who received Paul's revelation.
103. Did Paul preach a lawgiver or a Saviour?
104. What did Paul say about conferring?
105. Where did Paul go instead of to Jerusalem?
106. Does this verse indicate where the apostles were?
107. Do we have a record of Paul preaching in Arabia?
108. Where did he go after the trip to Arabia?
109. Did he preach in Damascus?
110. How was it received?

c) His visit to Jerusalem was not long enough for instruction in the gospel. 1:18-24

## Text 1:18-24

18 Then after three years I went up to Jerusalem to visit Cephas, and tarried with him fifteen days. 19 But other of the apostles saw I none, save James the Lord's brother. 20 Now touching the things which I write unto you, behold, before God, I lie not. 21 Then I came into the regions of Syria and Cilicia. 22 And I was still unknown by face unto the churches of Judaea which were in Christ: 23 but they only heard say, He that once persecuted us now preacheth the faith of which he once made havoc; 24 and they glorified God in me.

## Paraphrase

18 Then, after three years from my conversion, I went up to Jerusalem, to become acquainted with Peter; and being introduced to him by Barnabas, who knew how the Lord had appeared to me, I abode in his house fifteen days.

19 But, though I abode these days in Jerusalem, I saw no other of the apostles at that time, except James, the Lord's cousin-german.

20 Now, the things I write to you concerning myself, to shew that I am not an apostle of men, behold, in the presence of God I declare with assurance, I do not falsely represent them.

21 After the fifteen days were ended, I went first into the regions of Syria, and from thence into my native country Cilicia.

22 And I was personally unknown to the Christian churches in Judea; so that I could not receive either my commission or my doctrine from them.

23 But only they heard, that he who formerly persecuted the Christians, was become a zealous preacher of the facts concerning Christ which formerly he endeavoured to disprove.

24 And they praised God on account of my conversion, who had been so bitter an enemy to them.

## Comment 1:18

### then after three years I went up to Jerusalem

1. This is after his Arabian trip and his experience at Damascus of being close to a martyr's death.
2. Acts 9:26-30 tells of his trip there.
a. The disciples were afraid of him.
b. Barnabas told of Paul's conversion.
3. Paul then preached. going in and out of Jerusalem.

4. Grecian Jews sought to kill him, but the brethren helped him escape and he went to Tarsus.
5. The three years causes one to think of the apostles' three years of training under Christ. Some feel Paul was trained three years in Arabia.

**to visit Cephas** (alternate reading: "to get acquainted with Cephas")
1. Notice that he was preaching before he went to Jerusalem, and enemies sought to kill him there as in Damascus. Acts 9:26-29
2. Why were they not trying to kill Peter?
a. Probably because Peter was not giving the emphasis about Gentiles having equal rights as Paul was.
b. Probably because of Paul's radical change. Peter was of Galilee. Paul was one of them formerly and they turned on him.
c. The apostles seem to have been spared some persecution. Acts 8:2

**and tarried with him fifteen days**
1. This would be rather a brief time for instruction.
2. Jesus kept his disciples about three years; how could Paul expect to be qualified in fifteen days under Peter's teaching?

## Comment 1:19
**but other of the apostles saw I none**
1. Only two apostles were seen, so he could not have been instructed by all of them.
2. It is doubtful if James were an apostle as seen by the study unless by a special calling.
3. It seems Paul places him as an apostle, and that should settle it.

**James, the Lord's brother**
1. Is this James the author of the Book of James?
a. Yes, some say.
b. See McGarvey's *Evidences of Christianity*.
2. There were three James — and some say a fourth:
a. James, "the elder," son of Zebedee and brother of John, was one of the twelve (Matt. 10). He was martyred under Herod Agrippa in 44 A.D.
b. James, "the younger," son of Alphaeus was also an apostle (Matt. 10).

c. James, the brother of the Lord, is named in this text.

1) He is believed to have been a pillar in the church at Jerusalem. "James and Cephas and John, they who were reputed to be pillars, gave to me and Barnabas the right hand of fellowship, that we should go unto the Gentiles and they unto the circumcision." Gal. 2:9

2) He may have been made an apostle by a special appearance of the Lord. I Cor. 15:7 "then he appeared to James; then to all the apostles."

3) His judgment prevailed in the council at Jerusalem. Acts 15:13-29

4) According to Josephus he was stoned by order of Annas, the High Priest, about 63 A.D.

5) Some feel he was a cousin rather than a brother.

d. James the Less (Greek "little" — short of stature) is considered by some to be a fourth, but could be the same as (b.)

## Comment 1:20

**before God I lie not**

1. This amounts to an oath before God.

2. He was willing to call God's witness to the proof of his apostleship.

3. This is to establish the truthfulness of the history of his early experiences with the Lord.

## Comment 1:21

**the regions of Syria and Cilicia**

1. Paul's reasons for leaving Damascus are seen in Acts 9:22-25: the Jews took counsel to kill him. While in Jerusalem, he was in a trance and the Lord spoke: "And he said unto me, Depart: for I will send thee forth far hence unto the Gentiles." Acts 22: 17-21

2. Cilicia formed the part of Syria in Asia Minor, which part was separated from Syria proper by the high ridge of Mt. Taurus.

## Comment 1:22

**I was still unknown by face**

1. He had not held any meetings to give them a chance to become acquainted.

2. No doubt because of persecution, the Christians were not assembling in great meetings to hear this converted Jew.

## Comment 1:23

**But they only heard say**

1. He had a reputation that was second hand: they had not actually seen this former persecutor.
   a) Once he was a havoc maker.
   b) Now he preaches what he once destroyed.
2. Paul didn't have time to appear before all the scattered Christians.

## Comments 1:24

**they glorified God in me**

1. It was not because he urged circumcision and the law of Moses, but because he urged faith in Jesus Christ.
2. They rejoiced that an enemy was now a friend.

## Study Questions 1:18-24

111. How many years are named in this verse?
112. Was it three years after his Arabian trip, or was it three years after his conversion?
113. Could he have spent three years receiving instruction from Christ as did the other apostles?
114. Was Paul interested in any one disciple in Jerusalem?
115. Why was Peter's life in jeopardy, while Paul had already faced death?
116. Was fifteen days very long for Paul to receive instruction?
117. Why does Paul discuss the time element?
118. What apostles did Paul see?
119. Why were the others not seen?
120. Was the Lord's brother an apostle? Cf. also 1 Cor. 15:7
121. How many James' were there?
122. Was the Lord's brother the author of the book of James?
123. Did Paul feel that these words were extremely important? (vs. 20)
124. Who was called as a witness to the truth?
125. Where did Paul go from Jerusalem?
126. Locate his destination on a map.
127. Why did he leave Jerusalem?
128. Was Paul's face a familiar Christian face in Judea?
129. Why did the Christians not gather in great numbers to hear him?

130. Was Paul known to be a Christian?
131. What was reported concerning him?
132. Did all of them believe the report?
133. What is meant by glorifying God in Paul?
134. Do we glorify God in our preachers today?
135. If we speak against a preacher, how serious is it?

## Questions on Galatians, Chapter One

### True - False

_____ 1. Paul was an apostle of men and called by men.

_____ 2. This letter was sent to the people at Corinth from Galatia.

_____ 3. Paul was astonished that the brethren had removed from the faith.

_____ 4. A teacher of false doctrine should be considered as anathema.

_____ 5. Paul boasted to the Galatians that he had always been a minister of Christ.

_____ 6. Paul had been a zealous teacher of the Jewish traditions.

_____ 7. As widely as Paul traveled, it is strange that he never visited Arabia.

_____ 8. Paul says he visited Jerusalem after a three year period. (1:18)

_____ 9. Paul's stay at Jerusalem lasted 15 days.

_____10. While in Jerusalem Paul met most of the Apostles and was straightened out doctrinally.

_____11. The Galatian letter was directed to one Church in Galatia.

_____12. Only an angel from heaven had a right to change Paul's Gospel.

_____13. Paul stated that it was impossible to please all men and still be a servant of Christ.

_____14. Paul was chosen from his mother's womb.

_____15. Paul was not known by face to the Churches at Judea as stated in chapter.

_____16. Accursed, means to give over to the judgment of God.

_____17. Paul was very liberal with commendations as he begins the Galatian letter.

_____18. Paul was not chosen at the time Matthias was selected to take Judas' place, hence he was not an apostle.

_____19. Paul being reared in Tarsus and having Roman citizen-ship — was never very strong in the Jewish faith.

_____20. An apostle is one who rules over a large diocese.

_____21. Romans and Galatians do not show any resemblance doctrinally although they are from the same author.

_____22. Paul denies that he ever persecuted the Church.

_____23. The Galatians had their faults, but they never questioned Paul's apostleship.

_____24. Paul was driven from Damascus by persecution.

_____25. The Galatians were Gauls who were predominantly Irish.

_____26. Paul was advanced in religion beyond many of his own age.

## Questions on Galatians, Chapter One
### Completion

1. The Book of Galatians was written to the _____.
2. The author of the Book was _____.
3. The author marvels that they were so quickly_____.
4. The Book says the false teacher is to be _____.
5. Paul says the gospel he preached was not received of man, taught by man, but came to him through _____.
6. Paul says he did not confer with flesh and blood but went away into _____.
7. Paul says when he finally went up to Jerusalem he went up to visit _____.
8. Paul says that he persecuted the Church of _____.
9. When Paul made his short visit up to Jerusalem he says he saw none of the other apostles save _____.
10. The relative of the Lord that Paul saw was _____.

C. PAUL'S GOSPEL AND APOSTLESHIP CONFIRMED AND MAINTAINED. 2:1-21

1. Confirmed by the right hand of fellowship at Jerusalem. 2:1-10

### Text 2:1,2

**Then after the space of fourteen years I went up again to Jerusalem with Barnabas, taking Titus also with me. 2 And I went up by revelation: and I laid before them the gospel which I preach among the Gentiles but privately before them who were of repute, lest by any means I should be running, or had run, in vain.**

41

## Paraphrase

Then, within fourteen years from my conversion, I went up again to Jerusalem with Barnabas, taking with me Titus also, one of the idolatrous Gentiles whom I had converted.

2 And I then went up by the direction of Christ; and after declaring in public the success of my ministry, I explained to the apostles the gospel which I preach to the Gentiles: But to avoid offence, I did it privately to them who were of greatest reputation, namely, Peter, James, and John, lest perhaps, being suspected to preach differently from them, my future and past labours might become useless.

## Comment 2:1

### Then after the space of fourteen years

1. The connection with chapter one rather causes one to believe that this visit was fourteen years after his visit with Peter for fifteen days.
2. The question is raised then, about a second journey not mentioned here. This actually was Paul's third visit.
a. The second visit was during a time of great need — a famine. Cf. Acts 11:27-30 and 12:25
b. The second visit was at the time of a great persecution.
1) James, the brother of John, was killed with the sword. Acts 12:2
2) Peter was imprisoned. Acts 12:3
c. Barnabas was with him on the second visit.
3. There are several suggested theories concerning the fourteen years.
a. It was fourteen years from his first visit mentioned in 1:18.
b. It was fourteen years from his conversion.
c. It was fourteen years from the second visit mentioned in Acts 11:30 - 12:25.
1) Much is made of "Barnabas being with him." Cf. 11:30
2) Now in Galatians 2:1, he goes "up again to Jerusalem with Barnabas." It may be assumed that he is talking of fourteen years after his first trip with Barnabas.
3) Against this position it should be noted that it seems to have had no bearing on his apostleship.
a) Since it had no bearing on his apostleship, Paul makes no allusion to it.

b) Paul is referring back to 1:18 which did have a bearing on his apostleship.

4. Let us consider the history of this visit to Jerusalem .
a. It was made prior to Paul and Barnabas' separation. Acts 15:39
b. The trip to Jerusalem is known as The Jerusalem Conference. Acts 15
c. Following the visit, the brethren sent Judas (Barsabbas) and Silas back to Antioch with Paul and Barnabas, with a letter stating the convictions of the Jerusalem assembly.

**with Barnabas**

1. Why did Barnabas go with Paul to Jerusalem?
a. He had seen the results of Paul's preaching to the Gentiles.
b. The brethren appointed him to go. Acts 15:2
c. Barnabas had served to introduce Paul to the brethren who were afraid of him. Acts 9:26,27

2. Barnabas and Paul had formed a great evangelistic team.

**taking Titus also with me**

1. Reasons why Titus was taken:
a. He was a laborer with Paul, and he had worked among the churches in Crete.
b. He was a Gentile and would be proof that Gentiles need not practice Jewish rites.

2. The mention of these two men helped to identify the trip to Jerusalem.

## Comment 2:2

**and I went up by revelation**

1. Paul was ordered there by the Holy Spirit, although the agency was the church. Note this!

2. The church sent Paul for a specific purpose: "And certain men came down from Judæa and taught the brethren, saying, Except ye be circumcizsed after the custom of Moses, ye can not be saved. 2 And when Paul and Barnabas had no small dissension and questioning with them, the brethren appointed that Paul and Barnabas, and certain other of them, (Titus) should go up to Jerusalem unto the apostles and elders about this question." Acts 15:1,2

**I laid before them the gospel which I preach**

1. All that Acts states is, "And all the multitude kept silence;

and they hearkened unto Barnabas and Paul rehearsing what signs and wonders God had wrought among the Gentiles through them. Acts 15:12

2. It is not likely that he presented them with a copy of his sermons but that he orally rehearsed his convictions.

**but privately before them who were of repute**

1. Luther makes this read, "I conferred not only with the brethren, but with the leaders among them."
2. We should not do work in a community without the knowledge of the minister, or the elders.
a. It is a matter of respect to the faithful brethren already working there.
b. It appears then as unity rather than division.

**lest by any means I should be running, or had run in vain**

1. Paul had kept the Gentiles free from the yoke of the law and he did not want to undo all his work.
2. It had to be settled with the leaders or it would not be settled.

### Study Questions 2:1,2

136. What is meant by "space of fourteen years"?
137. Was this a second or third visit?
138. Who went with Paul?
139. Why did Barnabas go?
140. Explain the reason for the presence of Titus.
141. Was it Paul's idea to go to Jerusalem?
142. What was the nature of the revelation?
143. What did Paul do upon arrival?
144. What did he preach?
145. How was Paul received?
146. Who was present to hear Paul?
147. Discuss Paul's "running."

### Text 2:3-5

**3 But not even Titus who was with me, being a Greek, was compelled to be circumcised: 4 and that because of the false brethren privily brought in, who come in privily to spy out our liberty which we have in Christ Jesus, that they might bring us into bondage: 5 to whom we gave place in the way of subjection, no, not for an hour; that the truth of the gospel might continue with you.**

## *Paraphrase*

3 However, that the apostles to whom I communicated my gospel, acknowledged it to be the true gospel of Christ, is evident from this, that not even Titus, who was with me, though a converted Gentile, was compelled to be circumcised,

4 On account even of the secretly introduced false brethren of the Jewish nation, who, pretending to be Christians, came in privily to our meetings at Jerusalem, to find out and condemn our freedom from the law of Moses, which we Gentiles have obtained by Christ Jesus' gospel, that they might bring us into bondage under the law.

5 To these false brethren I did not give place, by subjecting Titus to the law of Moses, not even for an hour. This fortitude I shewed, that the truth of the gospel concerning the freedom of the Gentiles from that law might remain with you and all the Gentiles.

## Comment 2:3

### not even Titus . . . was compelled to be circumcised

1. The apostles were gathered and this was their decision, when the Pharisees said, "It is needful to circumcise them and to charge them to keep the law of Moses." Acts 15:5

a. Peter's word: "Now therefore why make ye trial of God, that ye should put a yoke upon the neck of the disciples which neither our fathers, nor we were able to bear?" Acts 15:10

b. James' word: "Wherefore my judgment is that we trouble not them that from among the Gentiles turn to God." Acts 15:19

c. The brethren's plan: They selected men out of their group to take a letter and to return to Antioch, Syria, and Cilicia. "For it seemeth good to the Holy Spirit and to us, to lay no greater burden than these necessary things." Acts 15:28

2. This was the apostles' big opportunity to condemn Paul's gospel but they did not; rather, they verified it.

3. Reasons why Paul then had Timothy circumcised: Acts 16:1-3

a. Titus was pure Gentile — Timothy was half Jew.

b. A background of Jewish religion made this problem a serious one. Now they could not use this as a stumbling block to his preaching.

c. Paul was a Jew and did not need to renounce all that was Jewish, for that would repel his people.

d. He became all things . . . to win some. I Cor. 9:20-23

## Comment 2:4

### And that because of the false brethren

1. Catholic Bible has a clearer reading: "although it was urged. on account of false brethren."
2. The Pharisees no doubt had a part. for they followed Christ and Paul everywhere to make trouble.

### privately brought in

1. Certainly the Apostles did not bring them in. No!
2. The trouble makers brought them in in secret.

### to spy out our liberty which we have in Christ

1. The Christian has freedom from the law of the O.T.
a. Paul in Romans uses the illustration of the woman whose husband dies: "Wherefore my brethren, ye also were made dead to the law through the body of Christ; that ye should be joined to another." Rom. 7:3; 7:4 Read also Gal. 5:1 Eph 6:8, Gal. 5:13.
2. Observe that liberty is in Christ only.
3. The Jews never gave up, for in later years Paul (in Jerusalem) took a vow with four others. Acts 21:21-26

### That they might bring us into bondage

1. The law was bondage compared to freedom in Christ. Gal. 4:3,4,5.
2. Instead of escaping from bondage. they wanted to bring others into it.

## Comment 2:5

### did not give way to subjection

1. Paul had Timothy circumcised because it was expedient in order to win the Jews. Acts 16:3
2. Here at Jerusalem—the action would set a precedent for all time.
3. The Gospel can not be comprised—we can not give way, or give place when it is God's place.
a) "Neither give place to the devil." Eph. 4:27
b) "Stand against the wiles of the devil." Eph. 6:11
c) Give not that which is holy unto the dogs. Matt. 7:6

**That the truth of the gospel might continue with you**

1. Either you have to become a Jew to become a Christian, or you do not. Paul said you do not, and stood his ground.
2. Either you are dead to the law or subject to it. Paul said you are not subject and would not give in.
a. "Wherefore my brethren ye also were made dead to the law through the body of Christ." Rom. 7:4
b. "So that the law is become our tutor to bring us unto Christ." Gal. 3:24

## Study Questions 2:3-5

148. How was Titus received?
149. Where is the subject of circumcision discussed more fully?
150. Why was Timothy circumcised?
151. Who was brought in?
152. Who would have done this?
153. Were they publicly brought in?
154. What is liberty in Christ?
155. Find other verses that deal with the subject.
156. Did the spies have evil motives?
157. What does Paul teach concerning bondage?
158. Did Paul compromise while in Jerusalem?
159. Did Paul ever give in to pressure?
160. Why was he so set in Jerusalem?
161. What is involved in the truth of the Gospel?

## Text 2:6-10

**6 But from those who were reputed to be somewhat (whatsoever they were, it maketh no matter to me: God accepteth not man's person)—they, I say, who were of repute imparted nothing to me: 7 but contrariwise, when they saw that I had been intrusted with the gospel of the uncircumcision, even as Peter with the gospel of the circumcision 8 (for he that wrought for Peter unto the apostleship of the circumcision wrought for me also unto the Gentiles): 9 and when they perceived the grace that was given unto me, James and Cephas and John, they who were reputed to be pillars, gave to me and Barnabas the right hands of fellowship, that we should go unto the Gentiles, and they unto the circumcision; 10 only they would that we should remember the poor; which very thing I was also zealous to do.**

## *Paraphrase*

6 Besides, from the greatest of the apostles I received nothing: Whatever they were during their attendance on Christ, is no lessening of me, as an apostle. God does not shew favour to men on account of external advantages. He did not raise them who attended Christ during his ministry, above me. For to me, they who were of greatest reputation communicated neither knowledge. nor spiritual gifts, nor authority: Far less did they pretend to make me an apostle.

7 But, on the contrary, perceiving by what Jesus said when he appeared to me, that the preaching of the gospel to the Gentiles was committed to me, even as the preaching of the gospel to the Jews had been committed to Peter;

8 For God, who wrought inwardly in Peter the gifts of inspiration, and miracles, and languages, to fit him for preaching to the Jews, wrought inwardly also in me the same gifts, in order to fit me for converting and instructing the Gentiles in every country whither I was to go.

9 And thus knowing the grace of apostleship which was bestowed on to me, James, and Peter, and John, who were esteemed chief supporters of the church, gave to me and Barnabas their right hands, in token of my fellowship with them in the apostolic office, and in token that Barnabas was sent forth by the Holy Ghost, to preach the gospel to the Gentiles; and agreed that we should travel among the Gentiles, while they preached to the Jews in Judea.

10 The only thing they desired was, that we would remember to make collectings for the poor, among the Gentiles; which very thing I also made haste to do among the converted Gentiles in Antioch.

## Comment 2:6

**But from those who were reputed to be somewhat**

1. The first ones chosen to be apostles would naturally carry much prestige.
2. No primacy of Peter is indicated here, although he must be referred to, as see in verse eight.

**whatsoever they were maketh no matter**

1. They could not rest upon their early calling.

2. Their prestige was not to be the deciding factor.
3. Truth, and not person of men, was to be the issue.

### they imparted nothing to me
1. Paul was not egotistical; he was simply stating that he had a revelation of the gospel, so how could men teach him?
2. He was blessed by their fellowship but the meeting was not to give Paul a message.

## Comment 2:7
### I had been intrusted with the gospel of the uncircumcision, even as Peter with the gospel of the circumcision
1. Are there two gospels? No.
2. Paul explains in verse eight what is meant: there is only one message.
3. It meant to whom the gospel was to be preached.

## Comment 2:8
### wrought for Peter unto the apostleship of circumcision
1. The gospel was to be preached first to the Jew. Rom. 1:16.
2. The apostles agreed on areas of service and Paul was to go to Gentiles. Gal. 2:9
3. It seems the words *gospel* and *apostleship* can be used interchangeably in verses seven and eight.

### wrought for me also unto the Gentiles
1. It is also translated "was mighty in me for the Gentiles."
2. Cf. Acts 9:15 "But the Lord said . . . 'He is a chosen vessel.'"

## Comment 2:9
### they perceived the grace that was given unto me
1. They could see:
a. The evidence of his salvation—the Holy Spirit.
b. The evidence of his own working of miracles.
c. The evidence of his own power in preaching.
2. Several verses using this same expression to show reference to Paul's apostleship. Cf. I Cor. 3:10; Rom. 12:3; Rom. 15:5

### James, Cephas and John
1. This James is believed to be the half-brother of Christ.
2. Notice that James is named first. There is no papal primacy here, or Peter's name would appear first.

### reputed to be pillars
1. Pillars are supports for the main building.
2. The strength of a local church is its local leadership as it

stands upon Christ, the bedrock.
a. Weak elders mean a sagging church.
b. The church is the pillar and ground of the truth. I Tim. 3:15
c. No nation is stronger than the church within it.

### Gave to me and Barnabas the right hands of fellowship

1. This is an open gesture of common acceptance.
2. "Strike hands is seen in the O.T."
a. Cf. Job 17:3 ". . . who is there that will strike hands with me."
b. Cf. Prov. 6:1 "My son, if thou are become surety for thy neighbor, if thou hast stricken thy hands, for a stranger . . ."

### That we should go unto the Gentiles and they unto the circumcision

1. This is the first comity agreement of the church.
2. The Gentiles have no special requirements given in this agreement.
3. This was to make certain a wide preaching of the Gospel.
a. This agreement was not among denominations to give all men a chance to hear the Gospel.
b. The gospel allows no favoritism.

## Comment 2:10

**only they would that we should remember the poor; which very thing I was also zealous to do.**

1. "The poor" probably referred to the Christians within the province of James, Peter, and John.
2. Paul's zeal to do this is evident both before and after the conference.
a. On his very first trip to Jerusalem, he took relief for the Judean brethren.
b. Cf. also
I Cor. 16:1; II Cor. 8:1-5; II Cor. 9:1-8; Rom. 15:25-27; Acts 24:17.

## Study Questions 2:6-10

162. Could the reputed ones refer to the primacy of Peter taught by some?
163. Was prestige more important to Paul than truth?
164. Did Paul receive any new truth from the reputed ones?
165. Does Paul teach that there are two gospels?
166. Did his preaching differ from Peter's?
167. Were Paul and Peter commissioned by the same authority?

168. Could the word "gospel" and "apostleship" refer to the same commission?
169. Could the gospels mentioned refer to areas of service rather than to content?
170. How did Paul decide that he was to go to the Gentiles?
171. Who perceived Paul's grace?
172. How was this grace manifested?
173. Who were the pillars?
174. How did the "pillars" react?
175. Did they agree on areas of work?
176. Is this comparable to comity agreements?
177. Who was the James named here?
178. If the men are named in order of importance, what does this do to the doctrine of the primacy of Peter?
179. What is the right hand of fellowship?
180. What exhortation was given to Paul's group?
181. Did Paul show interest in it?
182. Who would "poor" refer to?
183. Was Paul's word "zeal" well spoken?

2. Maintained in Conflict with Peter at Antioch. 2:11-21
a) The hypocritical conduct of Peter and the remainder of Jewish Christians. 2:11-13

### Text 2:11-13

**11 But when Cephas came to Antioch, I resisted him to the face, because he stood condemned. 12 For before that certain came from James, he ate with the Gentiles; but when they came, he drew back and separated himself, fearing them that were of the circumcision. 13 And the rest of the Jews dissembled likewise with him; insomuch that even Barnabas was carried away with their dissimulation.**

### Paraphrase

11 Moreover, to shew that as an apostle Peter is not superior to me, I inform you, that when he came to Antioch after the council, I opposed him personally in the presence of the church, because in this very affair of the Gentiles he was blamable.

12 For before certain persons zealous of the law came from James, he used to eat with the converted Gentiles in Antioch. But when they arrived, he withdrew, and separated himself from these, as if it had been a sin to eat with them. But the true reason was, his being afraid of the converted Jews.

13 And the other Jews also hypocrized with him, abstaining from the tables of the Gentiles. So that even Barnabas, who with me had preached salvation to the Gentiles without the works of the law, was carried away with them by their hypocrisy.

## Comment 2:11

**But when Cephas came to Antioch**

1. McGarvey feels this event probably was soon after the Jerusalem conference.
2. Observe that Peter is not named with Barsabbas and Silas who returned to Antioch from Jerusalem following the conference. Acts 15:22

**I resisted him to the face**

1. Paul spoke to his face—not behind his back, or in Peter's absence.
2. Resistance actually was upholding the truth.

**Because he stood condemned**

1. Notice it was Peter's conduct—an old prejudice showing forth.
2. This does not affect his revelation as inspiration.
a. These men who were given the keys of the kingdom were not given perfection.
b. They spoke a divine message but in normal life their prejudice entered into their application of it.

## Comment 2:12

**Before that certain came from James he ate with the Gentiles**

1. This was an unlawful act for the law enthusiasts.
   Cf. Samaritan woman—John 4:9 no dealing.
2. Peter's great vision (Acts 10:11-16) had some affect on him.
a. He had defended his position earlier, when the Jews contended with him when he returned to Jerusalem from the house of Cornelius. Acts 11
b. Now Paul records that in Antioch he again ate with Gentiles.
c. Peter was courageous when there was nothing to fear.

**when some came from James he drew back and separated**

1. This may represent then what he really believed.
a. He knew how they felt and since he had to deal more with them than the Christians at Antioch, he chose to be at peace with them.
b. This type of character Peter demonstrated in earlier life.
2. It would require some courage however to give up his position with the Gentiles.

3. Did James send them? Was he fearing James?
a. It is not likely if James remained true to his conviction at Jerusalem.
1) "Wherefore my judgment is, that we trouble not them that from among the Gentiles turned to God." Acts 15:19
2) "Forasmuch as we have heard that certain who went out from us have troubled you with words, subverting your souls; to whom we gave no commandment." Acts 15:24
b. The context somewhat infers that James is to blame.
1) If Peter could change, so could James.
2) The Pulpit Commentary says this is not inconsistent, for James could speak 15:19—and still feel that the obligation of Jewish believers remained the same.

## Comment 2:13

### The rest of the Jews dissembled
1. That is, the Jewish Christians began likewise breaking fellowship.
2. They acted as sheep without a shepherd.

### Even Barnabas was carried away with their dissimulation
1. Dissimulation—to dissemble—means "to feign, to make pretense of."
2. These men were supposed to be Christians and now they avoid the Gentiles at dinner. Paul says it is a pretense.
a. Dissimulation can be translated "hypocrisy."
b. To possess a truth and profess it in life are two different matters.

## Study Questions 2:11-13

184. Who is Cephas?
185. Where did he travel?
186. When did he make the trip?
187. What is meant by "resisted?"
188. How could an inspired apostle be wrong?
189. Do preachers today preach truth more strongly than they are able to live it?
190. What inconsistency did Peter show?
191. Had not Paul learned how to act toward Gentiles, according to Acts 10?
192. Why would the presence of James make a difference?
193. Was James a superior to Peter?

194. What is meant by "drew back and separated?"
195. Was James at fault or inconsistent?
196. What is meant by dissembled?
197. Who did it?
198. Was this a break in fellowship?
199. Is dissimulation hypocrisy?
200. Would it be inconsistent if we were present in a mixed foreign and colored group in a similar situation, if we had friends who were very strong in drawing color and social distinctions?

b. Paul's Reproof 2:14-21

## Text 2:14-16

**14 But when I saw that they walked not uprightly according to the truth of the gospel, I said unto Cephas before them all, If thou, being a Jew, livest as do the Gentiles, and not as do the Jews, how compellest thou the Gentiles to live as do the Jews?**

**15 We being Jews by nature, and not sinners of the Gentiles, 16 yet knowing that a man is not justified by the works of the law but through faith in Jesus Christ, even we believed on Christ Jesus, that we might be justified by faith in Christ, and not by the works of the law: because by the works of the law shall no flesh be justified.**

## Paraphrase

14 But when I saw that such eminent teachers did not walk rightly, according to their own knowledge of the true doctrine of the gospel, I said to Peter in the hearing of them all; in the hearing of Barnabas and all the Judaizers: If, in the house of Cornelius, thou, though thou art a Jew, livedest after the manner of the Gentiles in respect of meats, and not after the manner of the Jews, because thou knowest the truth respecting that matter, why now compellest thou the converted Gentiles to obey the law, by refusing to eat with them, as if the distinction of meats were necessary to their salvation?

15 I added, we apostles, who are Jews by birth and education, and not idolatrous Gentiles, who are ignorant of God, and of his will respecting the salvation of sinners,

16 Knowing by the law and the prophets, as well as by our own inspiration, that man is not justified by works of law, but only through the faith which Jesus Christ hath enjoined, even all

of us have believed in Jesus Christ, that we may be justified by the faith which Christ hath enjoined; and have not sought justification by works of the law. For by performing works of law, whether it be the law of nature or of Moses, no man shall be justified at the judgment.

## Comment 2:14
**I said unto Cephas before them all**
1. Here was a wholesale stampede and someone needed to bring soberness.
2. Paul had the courage to do it.
3. No doubt here was a history-making event.
4. Paul urged Timothy to do this type of thing. "them that sin rebuke in the sight of all, that the rest also may be in fear." I Tim. 5:20

**if thou being a Jew livest as a Gentile**
1. In what sense were those words meant?
a. Perhaps in the liberty of the gospel.
b. Perhaps in the eating of meat, after his vision.
c. Perhaps while living right there in Antioch, he had lived just like other Gentiles.
2. Pointed question—to point out an inconsistency.

**How compellest thou the Gentiles to live as do the Jews**
1. It is charge of inconsistency.
2. It is not fair for a Jew to accept a new position and ask then that those of the new position accept the old position.

## Comment 2:15
**We being Jews by nature, and not sinners of the Gentiles**
1. Here we are—Jews with all of our background, acknowledging the Gentiles, who are ordinarily considered sinners, as now acceptable to God. Why go back to the law? Why accept the gospel if it is not able to justify?
2. Sinners refers to the bigoted attitude.
3. This expression goes with what follows, not with what preceded.

## Comment 2:16
**Yet knowing that a man is not justified by work**
1. To justify literally means "to pronounce righteous;" not meaning that a man is righteous, but that God treats him as such.
2. The history of justification is traced in the Scriptures.
a. It was promised in Christ. "In Jehovah shall all the seed of

Israel be justified, and shall glory." Isaiah 45:25

"He shall see of the travail of his soul, and shall be satisfied: by the knowledge of himself shall my righteous servant justify many; and he shall bear their iniquities." Isaiah 53:11

b. It is an act of God.

1) "He is near that justifieth me." Is. 50:8
2) "Who shall lay anything to the charge of God's elect? It is God that justifieth." Rom. 8:33

c. It is not of works of the law.

1) "And by him everyone that believeth is justified from all things, from which ye could not be justified by the law of Moses." Acts 13:39
2) "For what the law could not do, in that it was weak through the flesh, God, sending his own Son in the likeness of sinful flesh and for sin, condemned sin in the flesh." Rom. 8:3
3) "Now that no man is justified by the law before God, is evident: for the righteous shall live by faith." Gal. 3:11

d. It is of grace.

1) "Being justified freely by his grace through the redemption that is in Christ Jesus." Rom. 3:24
2) "For this cause it is of faith, that it may be according to grace; to the end that the promise might be sure to all the seed; not to that only which is of the law." Rom. 4:16
3) "They that receive the abundance of Grace." Rom. 5:17-21

e. It comes by the death and resurrection of Christ.

1) "Who was delivered up for our trespasses, and was raised for our justification." Rom. 4:25
2) "And if Christ hath not been raised, your faith is vain; ye are yet in your sins." I Cor. 15:17
3) "Much more then, being now justified by his blood, shall we be saved from the wrath of God through him." Rom. 5:9

f. It entitles one to an inheritance.

"That being justified by his grace, we might be made heirs according to the hope of eternal life." Titus 3:7

### But through faith in Jesus Christ

1. What are we to believe about Him for justification?
a. Faith in His blood. Rom. 5:9
b. Faith in His Resurrection. Rom. 4:25 I Cor. 15:17
2. Good morals, if love and all other things fail.

**Even we believed on Christ Jesus, that we might be justified by faith**

1. All come the same way.
a. "If so be that God is one, and he shall justify the circumcision by faith, and uncircumcision through faith." Rom. 3:30
b. Paul had to be justified this way.
2. This eliminates the so called good moral one too.

**And not by the works of the law**

1. Is not of works Acts 13:39; Rom. 8:3; Gal. 3:11.
2. Is not of faith and works of the law united. Acts 15:1-29
a. "We reckon therefore that a man is justified by faith apart from the works of the law." Rom. 3:28
b. "But if it is by grace, it is no more of works." Rom. 11:6
c. "Ye are severed from Christ, ye who would be justified by the law; ye are fallen away from grace." Gal. 5:4

## Study Questions 2:14-16

201. Discuss Paul's charge of failure to live uprightly.
202. Whom did Paul address?
203. What is meant that Peter lived as a Gentile?
204. What is meant by compelling Gentiles to live as Jews?
205. Why did Paul make an open issue of it?
206. How could Paul be a Jew by nature?
207. What is meant by the expression "sinners"?
208. Does the expression go with what preceded or with the statement that follows?
209. Describe justification.
210. Is it a new word in the New Testament?
211. Are we made just by works?
212. Are we made just by living up to the law of Moses?
213. How are we justified by grace?
214. Will grace alone make us just?
215. How is the resurrection of Christ connected with Justification?
216. How is faith connected to justification?
217. If we have faith in the law and also works, could we be justified?

## Text 2:17-19

**17 But if, while we sought to be justified in Christ, we ourselves also were found sinners, is Christ a minister of sin? God forbid.**

**18 For if I build up again those things which I destroyed, I prove myself a transgressor.   19 For I through the law died unto the law, that I might live unto God.**

### Paraphrase

17 But if, while we apostles seek to be justified by the faith of Christ, even we ourselves are found sinners, by practising the rites of the law of Moses as necessary to salvation, contrary to our conscience, will Christ promote such iniquity, by justifying teachers who delude others in a matter of such importance? By no means.

18 For if we re-establish, by our practice, those rites as necessary to salvation, which, in our preaching, we declared not necessary, we certainly make ourselves transgressors by deceiving others.

19 Besides, to shew the folly of seeking to be justified by law. I told the Judaizers that we all, through breaking law, have died by the curse of law, so that if we live, we must live by the free gift of God, and not by law.

### Comment 2:17

#### But, if while we sought to be justified in Christ

1. We have turned our backs on the law as a means of justification.
a. Going back, as you have, shows a disappointment or a dissatisfaction in the justification which we have obtained.
b. We as apostles must not reveal a sinful attitude.
2. An example if bad, brings reproach on Christ and man.
a. We are saved by the works of the law or we aren't.
b. If we return to the law—what will be said of Christ?

#### Is Christ a minister of sin

1. If we are such sinners as to be unfit to be conversed with, or eaten with, then Christ can be accused as a minister of sin.
a. This is an explanation.
b. It is an unjust judgment to condemn Christ for man's failures.
2. Look here—if we the apostles favor this kind of an attitude which is sinful, then, we representing Christ, represent Him as a minister of sin.

### Comment 2:18

#### If I build up again . . . . , I prove myself a transgressor.

1. If you preach salvation through Christ, and then insist on

circumcision as a test of fellowship, you are building up what the gospel ended.

2. If you Build up what you destroyed—you are a sinner.

## Comment 2:19

### For I through the law died unto the law

1. How could he die to it, through it?
   "For as many of you as were baptized into Christ did put on Christ." Gal. 3:24-27
2. In the Christ of the law—which the law prepared for—Paul died to the law. "dead—through the body of Christ." Rom. 7:4
   a. The law brought men to Christ. Gal. 3:24
   b. Therefore in accepting the fulfillment of the law, Paul died to the law.

### That I might live unto God

1. It did not loose him from duty but bound to a greater one.
   a. Rom. 6:1-5
   b. "Wherefore, my brethren, ye also were made dead to the law through the body of Christ; that ye should be joined to another, even to him who was raised from the dead, that we might bring forth fruit unto God." Rom. 7:4
2. This life unto God is unique:
   I give Him my burdens,
   He gives me His BLESSINGS.
   I give Him my trials,
   He gives me His PATIENCE.
   I give Him my sorrow,
   He gives me His STRENGTH.
   I give Him my blindness,
   He gives me His LIGHT.
   I give Him my cold heart,
   He gives me His LOVE.
   I give Christ my all,
   And He gives me HEAVEN.

## Study Questions 2:17-19

218. If a person follows the law, what is he doing to Christ?
219. Does a Christian's sins make Christ a minister of sin?
220. What is the special application of this verse to the Christian?
221. What is meant by "build up again?"

222. What had the gospel ended?
223. What had Paul destroyed?
224. Is the Gentile Christian today dead to the law of Moses?
225. By what process did Paul, a Jew, die to it?
226. What is the purpose of dying unto the law?
227. In what relationship are we to live, when we die to sin?

## Text 2:20-21

**20 I have been crucified with Christ, and it is no longer I that live, but Christ liveth in me: and that life which I now live in the flesh I live in faith, the faith which is in the Son of God, who loved me, and gave himself up for me. 21 I do not make void the grace of God: for if righteousness is through the law, then Christ died for naught.**

## Paraphrase

20 To prove that we die through law, I observed, that by the curse of law we are crucified together with Christ; Nevertheless we believers still live; only it is no longer the old man, with the affections and lusts, but Christ who liveth in us. For the life which we now live in the body, after the crucifixion of our old man, we live by that faith which is enjoined of the Son of God, who loved us, and give himself to death for us, that he might rule us, and obtain pardon for us.

21 I do not, like the Judaizers, set aside the mercy of God in giving his Son, by teaching justification through works of law. For if righteousness is attainable through law, then certainly Christ hath died in vain. He need not have died to deliver us from the curse, and to obtain eternal life for us.

## Comment 2:20

### For I have been crucified with Christ

1. Paul in Romans enlarges on this idea. "We were buried therefore with him through baptism into death . . . knowing this, that our old man was crucified with him, that the body of sin might be done away, that so we should no longer be in bondage to sin." Rom. 6:4,6

2. Too many in the church today are not crucified with Christ.
a. Sample of ones not crucified:
TIRED CHRISTIANS: Will work if coaxed.
RE-TIRED CHRISTIANS: Believe they have done their share and sit idly by, exercising the right to criticize.

RUBBER-TIRED CHRISTIANS: Go along all right if the way is smooth and the way clear.

FLAT-TIRED CHRISTIANS: Once were closely affiliated with the Church but suffered a puncture of ego and have never recovered.

AT-TIRED CHRISTIANS: Go to church on Easter and other times to show off new clothes.

TIRE-LESS CHRISTIANS: Always on the job and fully consecrated to the Lord Jesus Christ.

WHAT KIND OF A CHRISTIAN ARE YOU?

b. Typical Christians who are not crucified:

ONE CROSS—Nearly new. I cannot carry it and keep up with the world at the same time.

ONE TALENT—Unused, but shelfworn. It has been hidden away for years.

ONE SET OF CHRISTIAN ARMOR—Five pieces. This set needs polishing, but there is not a scratch or scar on it.

ONE PRAYING KNEE—Wholly unused since the limb sprouted a dancing foot.

ONE BIBLE—The pages of the family record have been used, other wise good as new.

ONE THOUSAND OPPORTUNITIES—Most of these are gone, but there may be a few good ones left. These many articles are stored in my attic.

### It is no longer I that live, but Christ that liveth in me

1. He has been crucified—yet he lives.
a. He is yet a living person.
b. He does not say that it ends his existence.
2. He means that in this new life, one lives in Him.
a. Christ lives in him as Saviour.
b. Christ lives in him as a guide.
c. Christ lives in him as one sensitive to sin.
d. Christ lives in him as a strengthening one. Phil. 4:13

### The life that I live in the flesh, I live in faith

1. The Christian life is a believing life.
a. Believing that I am saved. John 3:16
b. Believing that God will care. "To them that love God all things work together for good, even to them that are called." Rom. 8:28

c. Believing in a new body. I Cor. 15
a. A glorified body.
b. An eternal body.
c. A body without pain. Rev. 20:4
2. Paul proved that a person in the flesh could live in the Spirit.

### The faith which is in the Son of God

1. Faith is in a person—not a law.
2. Salvation is in Christ. not in observances.

### who loved me

1. Jesus had much to say about the Father's love—very little of his own love—thus he gave the credit to God.
2. John records Jesus' references to His own love.
a. "A new commandment I give unto you, that ye love one another; even as I have loved you, that ye also love one another." John 13:34
b. "Even as the Father hath loved me, I also have loved you: abide ye in my love." John 15:9
c. "This is my commandment, that ye love one another, even as I loved you." John 15:12
d. It was Jesus who spoke the message of love in John 3:16.

### and gave Himself up for me

1. Christ lived a life of love and compassion.
2. He died for man as an indication of His love.
a. "Greater love hath no man than this." John 15:13
b. "And to know the love of Christ which passeth knowledge, that ye may be filled unto all the fulness of God." Eph. 3:19
c. "And walk in love even as Christ also loved you and gave himself for us, an offering and a sacrifice to God for an odor of sweet smell." Eph. 5:2
3. Do we practice what we sing. This will answer the question, "What will we give up for Christ?"
   "I Love to Hear the Story."
   —if it doesn't last over 20 minutes.
   "Take My Life and Let it Be,"
   —Yes, let it be, dear Lord.
   "Sweet Hour of Prayer,"
   —is wonderful, but I'm really too busy.
   "I Love to Hear the Story,"
   —but only in Church.

"Have Thine Own Way, Lord,"
—with Mrs. Gray and Mrs. Black.
"Lead Me to Some Soul Today,"
—but wait until I have a convenient time.
"All I have is Thine Own,"
—but I hope that You don't mind that I have used it all for something which I want.
"If Jesus Goes with Me,"
—it may be embarrassing for both of us.

## Comment 2:21

### I do not make void the grace of God

(Catholic translation—"I do not cast away the grace of God".)

1. This is a charge against Peter: "You do by your action."
2. "But if it is by grace, it is no more of works: otherwise grace is no more grace." Rom. 11:6
3. The law was God's grace to bring us to Christ, who is God's complete demonstration of grace.

### if righteousness is through the law, then Christ died for naught

1. Jesus just wasted His time if righteousness can be obtained some other way.
2. Note how people think that they obtain righteousness today:
a. Indulgences
b. Masses

## Study Questions 2:20-21

228. What does Paul mean by crucifixion with Christ?
229. In what way or ways are we no longer ourselves?
230. Did Paul mean that he was no longer responsible for his life?
231. How does Christ live in man?
232. In whom is our faith?
233. Is there a difference in faith in a person and faith in a law?
234. How did Christ demonstrate His love for us?
235. Is Paul insinuating that Peter made God's grace void, when he says that he doesn't?
236. Would Christ's life have been necessary if grace were from any other source?
237. What is meant by the word "righteousness?"
238. By what means do people seek to obtain salvation today?

## Questions on Galatians, Chapter Two
### Choice:

1. Barnabas had the respect of the brethren in
    1. Alexandria
    2. Tarsus
    3. Jerusalem

2. Paul went up to Jerusalem
    1. to attend the feast of Pentecost
    2. because he was told to do so by Revelation
    3. on the back of a mule

3. Titus was like Timothy
    1. half Jew
    2. a hardened Jew
    3. a convert to Christianity

4. The apostles gave to Paul
    1. the right hand of fellowship
    2. an offering for the poor in Antioch
    3. a copy of the Old Testament

5. Paul took with him to Jerusalem
    1. Titus
    2. James
    3. Cephas

6. Because of the Council at Jerusalem not even
    1. Paul
    2. Titus
    3. Cephas
was compelled to be circumcised.

7. When Peter came to Antioch Paul
    1. resisted Peter face to face
    2. congratulated him for coming
    3. took up an offering to help him return to Jerusalem.

8. If Paul were to build up again those things which he destroyed he would become
    1. more consecrated as a Christian
    2. a Sadducee
    3. a transgressor

9. Paul took Barnabas with him to Jerusalem because
    1. Barnabas knew the way
    2. Barnabas could act as a mediator for Paul
    3. Barnabas begged to go

10. By the works of the law
    1. some will be justified
    2. the Jew will be justified
    3. none will be justified

11. Paul said he gave place in the way of subjection
    1. no not for an hour
    2. because of expediency
    3. to avoid strife

12. Paul was charged to remember the poor
    1. which thing he was zealous to do
    2. because there were so many of them
    3. because Paul had not shown much interest

13. Pillars in the Jerusalem Church were
    1. Matthew and Alpheaus
    2. James and Cephas
    3. Andrew and Peter

14. The rest of the Jews dissembled likewise means
    1. they broke fellowship
    2. they had a recess
    3. they assembled in a body

15. Paul says if righteousness is through the law
    1. then Gentiles had better get busy
    2. the Jew had an obligation to preach it
    3. then Christ died for naught. (vs. 21)

16. Paul said that he had been crucified
    1. with the cruelest of men
    2. with the same kind of a cross as Christ
    3. with Christ

17. During the Jerusalem conference, false brethren came in to
    1. spy out our liberty
    2. to insist that all Jews leave the conference
    3. to steal the offering for the poor
    4. to question Paul's baptism

18. Paul preached the gospel privately in Jerusalem because
    1. he might be killed
    2. he was afraid
    3. lest he should be running in vain

19. Paul speaks of making a trip to Jerusalem
      1. 14 years later
      2. to rebuke Peter
      3. because he was anxious to see the brethren
20. With Paul were
      1. Jonathan and Erasmus
      2. Phoebe and Prisca
      3. Barnabas and Titus
21. Titus in nationality
      1. was a Roman
      2. Jew
      3. Greek
22. James, John, Peter when they saw the favor of God in Paul
      1. turned them away resentfully
      2. extended the right hand of fellowship
      3. were jealous because he was not one of the twelve.
23. Paul said that he, because of the apostle Peter's attitude
      1. opposed him face to face
      2. grew to deeply appreciate him
      3. couldn't help but admire him
      4. was convinced of Peter's greatness

PART TWO

# JUSTIFICATION: NOT BY LAW BUT BY FAITH IN CHRIST
# 3:1 - 4:31

## A. JUSTIFICATION BY FAITH PROVED. 3:1-14
1. By reception of the Holy Spirit 3:1-5

### Text 3:1-5

**1 O foolish Galatians, who did bewitch you, before whose eyes Jesus Christ was openly set forth crucified? 2 This only would I learn from you, Received ye the Spirit by the works of the law, or by the hearing of faith? 3 Are ye so foolish? having begun in the Spirit, are ye now perfected in the flesh? 4 Did ye suffer so many things in vain? if it be indeed in vain. 5 He therefore that supplieth to you the Spirit, and worketh miracles among you, doeth he it by the works of the law, or by the hearing of faith?**

### Paraphrase

1 The doctrine of justification by faith is so full of comfort, and the proofs of it are so clear, that I must ask you, O senseless Galatians, what false teacher hath deceived you, and turned you from the gospel, to whom plainly Jesus Christ was set forth crucified for you, in order to procure you eternal life?

2 This only would I ask you who are gone over to Judaism, On account of performing the works of the law of Moses, received ye from me the gifts of the Spirit, whereby your acceptance with God was sealed? Or on account of your yielding the obedience of faith? When I communicated the gifts of the Spirit to you, few of you had any knowledge of the law of Moses.

3 Are ye so senseless, that having begun to live acceptably to God under the gospel, ye now attempt to make yourselves perfect in point of acceptance by performing the rites of the law of Moses ,whose only use is to purify the flesh?

4 Have ye suffered so many evils for the gospel to no purpose? seeing indeed it is to no purpose to have suffered them, if ye seek justification by the law of Moses; for in that case, the gospel will be of no advantage to you.

5 He, then, who communicated to you the gifts of the Spirit, and who wrought miracles among you, did he these things on account of recommending the works of the law of Moses, as necessary to your justification? or on account of recommending the obedience of faith to you, as the means of your salvation?

## Comment 3:1

### o foolish Galatians

1. Here he does not call them brethren but foolish people.
a. They had listened to false teaching.
b. They were returning to bondage.
2. What a person believes does make a difference according to the word of God.
a. Cf. I Cor. 1:10-13 where division is condemned.
b. Cf. John 10:16 and 17:20-21 where Christ speaks of oneness.
3. Foolish people risk the danger of coming short of God's rest. Cf. Heb. 4:1; Heb. 2:1; 3:12

### who did bewitch you

1. The implied answer is "Satan."
2. He points out that this is a fruit of the flesh.
3. Idolatry and Witchcraft are also bewitching. Gal. 5:20
4. Following false teaching surely classifies one in the realm of foolishness.

### that ye should not obey the truth

1. This phrase does not appear in the American Standard version.

2. The Catholic Bible—revision of the Challoner Rheims version —in the footnote says "Some Vulgate codices and the Clementine edition add "That you should not obey the truth." p. 516.

**before whose eyes Jesus Christ was openly set forth.**

1. Was he crucified where they could see Him?
a. Such was not likely: no doubt none, or very few, were present at the crucifixion.
b. The Catholic Bible says "been depicted crucified."
2. It may mean Paul had portrayed the crucifixion until they´saw it clearly enough to believe and obey.
a. It was set before them in preaching.
b. It was set before them through the spreading of the Lord's Table.
3. Was something set forth before Paul's eyes? Not likely.
a. Paul's eyes beheld two things if this view is accepted:
1) Christ crucified
2) Galatians bewitched
b. Of course this could be in a figurative sense, but it is not the teaching of the text.

**crucified** or "Crucified among you"—Luther.

1. Perhaps he says they have recrucified Jesus.
a. "Seeing they crucify to themselves the Son of God afresh, and put him to an open shame." Heb. 6:6
b. In the light of Heb. 6:6 this is not an impossible interpretation of Luther's.
2. This would be a serious charge to these brethren.

## Comment 3:2

**this only would I learn from you.**

1. "Let me ask you one question; that is enough to settle the question."
2. This expression shows Paul's great concern.

**received ye the Spirit.**

1. Yes, they did receive personally the indwelling presence.
a. "And because ye are sons God sent forth the Spirit of his Son into our hearts, crying, Abba, Father." Gal. 4:6
b. This should prove the inferiority of the law.
2. Yes, they did, for some of them were able to work miracles. (Gal. 3:5)

**by the works of the law or by the hearing of faith.**

1. Name the proper answer and you will see wherein is the approval of God.
2. They began in the Spirit, now they are trying to perfect themselves in the flesh.
3. The hearing of faith brought them the Spirit; now why go back to the law that did not and could not bring them the Spirit of God.

## Comment 3:3

**having begun in the Spirit are ye now perfected in the flesh?**

1. This is advancing backward, Paul says.
a. Note that Paul in 4:1-6 says "law" then "Christ."
b. Here he says your step has been Christ and now law.
2. They have begun in the Spirit — with power, miracles, liberties, grace. Now they have turned to perfect their life by fleshly rites, forms, ordinances.
3. How do we perfect ourselves? Let the Scriptures answer.
a. By study of the Word. II Tim. 3:16-17
b. ". . . that they may be perfected into one; that the world may know that thou didst sent me, and lovedst them even as thou lovedst me." John 17:23
c. By being transformed. Rom. 12:2

## Comment 3:4

**did ye suffer so many things in vain? If it be indeed in vain.**

1. You embraced the Christian doctrine and suffered for it.
2. Your folly is greater if you desert it now.
3. To forsake Christ after your vision of His is a shameful thing.
a. You could have escaped sufferings altogether by embracing Judaism in the first place, for the Jews are not persecuted.
b. The Jews stirred up the hostility of Gentiles.
4. McGarvey says it may be translated "If indeed it is only in vain."
a. Here Paul would mean he hopes that the reward of suffering would not extend to the loss of salvation.
b. This, McGarvey feels, is forceful, but a strained interpretation. p. 265
5. McGarvey feels that actually Paul is expressing a hope that they may repent of their apostasy and so not lose the reward of their sufferings. Cf. Matt. 5:11-12

## Comment 3:5

**he therefore that supplieth to you the Spirit**

1. Who is the He?
a. No doubt it is God — for it is God back of the person even if a person is meant.
1) "For it is God who worketh in you both to will and to work, for his good pleasure." Phil. 2:13
2) The Spirit comes to the believer in faith and obedience, therefore God supplies the Spirit.
b. This verse itself indicates that Deity is involved for it is the hearing of faith that causes the Spirit to be supplied.
2. Paul could mean self: "And when Paul had laid his hands upon them the Holy Spirit came on them; and they spake with tongues, and prophesied." Acts 19:6

**and worketh miracles among you.**

1. Paul had.
a. At Lystra, he made a cripple (from mothers womb) walk. They called Barabas, Jupiter, and Paul, Mercury. Acts 14:8
b. Paul was stoned and left for dead, but arose. Acts 14:19
2. McGarvey feels that "He" refers to God, rather than to God's minister who worked miracles.

**doeth he it by the works of the law, or by the hearing of faith?**

1. God had not worked miracles among them at the hand of the Jews, but by men who preached the Gospel.
2. It came by their belief and so their case was like Abraham's.

## Study Questions 3:1-5

239. How does Paul address the Galatians in this chapter?
240. In what way had they become fools?
241. What does "bewitch" mean?
242. Are we bewitched if we follow false teachers?
243. Is it possible to be obedient to truth and yet practice false doctrines at the same time?
244. Did these converts see Christ's crucifixion?
245. How could Paul have meant it?
246. Is it possible that he meant that they had crucified Christ?
247. If false teaching crucifies Christ, has a false teacher any right to expect salvation?
248. What did Paul want to learn?
249. Had they received the Spirit?

250. When did they receive the Spirit — after they gave up the law or before?
251. If faith brings the Spirit, what would be the advantage of returning to the law?
252. Of what foolishness are they accused?
253. Is the law of Moses a perfecting instrument?
254. If we begin in Christ, are we to end in Him too?
255. What had they suffered?
256. Why had they suffered?
257. Is suffering for righteousness in vain?
258. Identify the supplier here.
259. Who worked miracles among them?
260. Is the miracle worker and supplier, the apostle Paul?
261. What is the record of Paul's miracles?

2. Justification by faith proved by the case of Abraham. 3:6-9

### Text 3:6-9

**6 Even as Abraham believed God, and it was reckoned unto him for righteousness. 7 Know therefore that they that are of faith, the same are sons of Abraham. 8 And the scripture, foreseeing that God would justify the Gentiles by faith, preached the gospel beforehand unto Abraham, saying, In thee shall all the nations be blessed. 9 So then they that are of faith are blessed with the faithful Abraham.**

### Paraphrase

6 That both Jews and Gentiles are to be justified by faith, is evident: For seeing Abraham believed God, and it (his believing) was counted to him for righteousness,

7 Know ye certainly, that they who imitate Abraham in his faith, and who seek to be justified, as he was, by faith, the same are the sons of Abraham, to whom the promises were made; and particularly the promise, that their faith shall be counted to them for righteousness.

8 For God, the author of the scripture, having predetermined that he would justify the nations by faith, preached the good news to Abraham before the law was given, and even before Abraham was circumcised; saying Gen. 12:3. Surely in thee all the nations of the earth shall be blessed with the blessing of justification by faith.

9 Wherefore, according to God's promises, they who imitate Abraham in his faith, and who after his example seek to be justified by faith, shall be blessed with believing Abraham, by having their faith counted to them for righteousness.

## Comment 3:6

### Even as Abraham believed in God

1. The Scriptures tell of Abraham's faith.
a. "And he believed in Jehovah; and he reckoned it to him for righteousness." Gen. 15:6
b. "For what saith the Scripture? And Abraham believed God . . ." Romans 4:3
c. He received it while in uncircumcision. Romans 4:9-10
d. He received it after he had been reckoned as righteous — as a seal. 4:11
2. We have a different seal as Christians.
a. "Howbeit the firm foundation of God standeth, having this seal, The Lord knoweth them that are his." II Tim. 2:19
1) The blessings bestowed shows He knows.
2) The answer to prayers shows He knows.
b. "Who also sealed us, and gave us the earnest of the Spirit in our hearts." II Cor. 1:22
c. "In whom ye also . . . having also believed, ye were sealed with the Holy Spirit of promise." Eph. 1:13
d. "And grieve not the Holy Spirit of God, in whom ye were sealed unto the day of redemption." Eph. 4:30
3. The case of Abraham antedated the law by 430 years according to Gal. 3:17.

### it was reckoned unto him for righteousness.

1. Since Abraham by faith would work with God, God could work with him as a righteous one.
2. The prime requirement is faith and not law.

## Comment 3:7

### they that are of faith, are the sons of Abraham

1. We are saved by faith and not genealogically.
2. By faith Abraham came into proper relationship with God. He was a child of God.
3. We become a son of Abraham and, of course, a son of God by faith.

## Comment 3:8

**and the scripture forseeing**

1. What is meant by forseeing?
a. It means the event was foretold.
b. Scripture is always in advance of man's wisdom.
2. How long before did they forsee?
a. 430 years before the law, the scriptures told of the faith that would justify the Gentiles.
b. The blind Jews had veiled this truth from the Galatians.

**preached the Gospel beforehand unto Abraham**

1. The gospel preached was good tidings, that all the families of the earth would be blessed.
2. All families means all nations.
3. Observe that the King James says, "Preached before the Gospel."
a. This does not change the meaning.
b. Read it with a comma after the word before.
c. Note that the context likewise agrees with A. S. V.

**in thee shall all the nations be blessed**

1. This is expressed in Gen. 12:3.
2. The blessing would come by faith; and faith would be in the person of Christ.
3. The law was to prepare the way; it was not the way.
4. Now 430 before the law and 1500 years of law have gone by and in the fulness of time (Gal. 4:4) the person of Christ has performed this.

## Comment 3:9

**they that are of faith are blessed with the faithful Abraham**

1. Everyone can be of faith.
a. Those who were not of genealogical fortune, were unfortunate under the law.
b. Everyone can be under the blessing of Abraham by faith.
c. The "whosoever" of John 3:16 is all inclusive.
2. What was the blessing of Abraham?
a. The blessing of righteousness—justification imputed to Abraham is now imputed to Gentile men of faith.
b. The God who blessed Abraham abundantly is the same God today.

## Study Questions 3:6-9

262. What Patriarch is used as an example of faith rather than works?
263. How many years prior to their time was Abraham?
264. By how many years did his father precede the law?
265. By what evidence was Abraham's faith accepted?
266. Did the Galatians have evidence that their faith was acceptable?
267. Define the word "reckoned".
268. Were the Galatians children of Abraham?
269. Are Gentile Christians today his children too?
270. Why is faith so exalted by the apostle here, as though obedience is not necessary?
271. Define forseeing.
272. Who should have seen through the eyes of Scripture?
273. How did Abraham hear the gospel?
274. How could Abraham bless all the nations?
275. Was this blessing only for the nations of his day?
276. Does the blessing cut across national and genealogical lines?
277. What blessing of Abraham will we receive?
278. Who is meant by "they that are of faith"?

3. Justification by faith proved by the inability of the Law to Justify. 3:10-12

### Text 3:10-12

**10 For as many as are of the works of the law are under a curse: for it is written, Cursed is every one who continueth not in all things that are written in the book of the law, to do them. 11 Now that no man is justified by the law before God, is evident: for, The righteous shall live by faith; 12 and the law is not of faith; but, He that doeth them shall live in them.**

### Paraphrase

10 But all, without exception, who seek justification by the works of the law of Moses, whether moral or ceremonial, instead of obtaining the blessing of justification, are under the curse of that law: For it is written, Most severely to be punished is every one, who doth not continue in all the precepts written in the book of the law of Moses, to do them.

11 Besides, that by works of law no one can be justified before God, is manifest from Habakkuk, who hath said nothing of men's

being just by works, but hath declared, (Ch. 2:4), that the just by faith shall live eternally.

12 Also, the law of Moses doth not require faith as the means of obtaining life eternal. But it saith. He who doth these things. the judgments and ordiances of God. mentioned in Lev. 18 shall live by them a long and happy life in Canaan.

## Comment 3:10

**as many as are of the works of the law are under a curse**

1. The blessing of justification comes by faith.
2. Those under the law could not be justified. for all failed to keep it, thus they rested under a curse.
3. Would this not be a contradiction to Romans 2:13 "For not he hearers of the law are just before God but the doers of the law shall be justified"?
a. No, for in Romans he is emphasizing that the Gentile was a responsible person.
b. Though his law was inferior to the Jewish law, yet he would be bound by it.
4. Now history has passed on — the law is no longer binding on the Jew.

**for it is written**

1. This is a quotation from Deuteronomy 27:26.
2. This quotation from the law itself should settle the issue.

**cursed is every one who continueth not in all things that are written in the book of the law to do them**

1. No man could live up to the law — hence all were cursed.
2. Even the rich young ruler was not an exception. Luke 18:18-23
a. He broke the law of covetousness.
b. The law, while sounding simple. is too profound for complete observance.

## Comment 3:11

**now that no man is justified by the law before God is evident**

1. What is the evidence?
a. The evidence is expressed in the remainder of the verse "For the righteous shall live by faith."
b. This evidence here is only a summary—it has a great meaning.
2. The brief summary is that the law itself curses righteousness by the law.

**for the righteous shall live by faith**

1. This is a quotation and is repeated elsewhere: Hebrews 2:4 and Romans 1:17
2. This evidence is seen in at least three ways.
a. The history of faith is evidence.
1) Abraham is an example. Gen. 12
2) Abel is an example. Heb. 11:4 (offered sacrifice)
3) Enoch is an example. Heb. 11:5 (was translated)
4) Noah is an example. Heb. 11:7 (built an ark)
b. It is evident in dealing with God that work is worth nothing without faith.
1) "Without faith it is impossible to be well-pleasing unto him." Heb. 11:6
2) Cain is an example — his sacrifice represented as much work, but it was not acceptable.
3) The prophets cried out against faithless sacrifices: Hosea 12:11 and Amos 5:21
c. It is evident in the fact that faith is the inspirer of acceptable works.
1) "If ye love me, ye will keep my commandments." John 14:15
2) "For in Christ Jesus neither circumcision nor uncircumcision; but faith working through love." Gal. 5:6
3) "Depart from me ye cursed." Matt. 25:41
3. Read this text again as follows. "The just by faith shall live."

## Comment 3:12

**and the law is not of faith**

1. The Catholic Bible reads "Law does not rest on faith."
2. A logical question to ask is "What is it of?"
a. Actually the law was a governmental system for a body of Jewish slaves, set free from Egypt.
1) They needed no law under Egypt when they were under Egyptian law.
2) The law helped to make them a nation and to bind them as a nation to God.
b. The law was their teacher.
3. With the law it was not so much "What do you believe?" as "What have you done?"
a. It required obedience and a daily punishment for those who broke it.

b. Its punishment and reward was immediate while faith like Abraham's looked more to the future.

**but, He that doeth them shall live in them**

1. If you were obedient, you were permitted to live, but disobedience brought death.

a. Lev. 18:5 is quoted in verse 12 with the implication of death if not kept.

b. "For everyone that curseth his father or his mother shall surely be put to death: he hath cursed his father or his mother; his blood shall be upon him." Lev. 20:9

c. "The adulterer and adultress shall surely be put to death." Lev. 20:10

d. "The ox shall be stoned, and its owner also shall be put to death." Exodus 21:29

e. A disobedient son is to be stoned. Deut. 21:18-21

2. The following are some examples of death:

a. At the hand of God.

1) Korah. Numbers 16:32

2) Teasing children. II Kings 2:24

b. At the hands of the elders

1) Achan. Joshua 7:18

2) Naboth. I Kings 21:8-14

## Study Questions 3:10-12

279. What constitutes being "of the works of the law"?

280. Do we have people guilty of it today?

281. How much of the law does one need to practice to be under the law?

282. Define the curse.

283. What text did Paul quote to prove his point?

284. The rich young ruler claimed to have kept the law perfectly, but what law had he broken?

285. Did this one thing bring him under the curse?

286. What does he mean "is evident"?

287. What is evidence?

288. Why cannot people see it — if the evidence is present?

289. Will a man live more righteously by faith than by law?

290. What have men been caused to do by faith?

291. Is work displeasing to God when it is done without faith? Give example.

292. Did the prophets speak similarly to Paul in regard to faith and work?
293. What is meant by "law is not of faith"?
294. What is the law "of", if it is not of faith?
295. What did the law propose to do?
296. Was the punishment of the law immediate?
297. Give some examples of its strictness and its penalties.
298. Explain what is meant by the idea that you could live if you obeyed the law.

4. Justification by faith proved by the death of Christ on the Cross. 3:13-14

## Text 3:13-14

**13 Christ redeemed us from the curse of the law, having become a curse for us; for it is written, Cursed is every one that hangeth on a tree:   14 that upon the Gentiles might come the blessing of Abraham in Christ Jesus; that we might receive the promise of the Spirit through faith.**

## Paraphrase

13 Wherefore, justification according to the tenor, whether of the law of nature or of the law of Moses, being a thing impossible in our present sinful state, Christ, ever since the fall, hath bought us all off from the curse of the law; consequently hath bought us off from law itself, as a rule of justification; having become an accursed person, a person most ignominiously punished for us: for it is written, Most ignominiously punished in every one who is hanged on a tree.

14 This deliverance Christ hath wrought, that the blessing of justification by faith, promised to Abraham, might come on the nations through Christ Jesus, Abraham's seed; and that we Gentiles might receive the promised gifts of the Spirit through faith, as the evidence of our being justified by faith, and of our being the sons of God.

## Comment 3:13

### Christ redeemed us from the curse of the law
1. What was the curse of the law?
a. The curse followed a break of the law.
b. All men broke the law, so as long as men lived under the law the curse hung over them.

c. The curse is the wrath of God: banishment from God and death.

2. The important thing is to see the liberation obtained by Christ.

a. Under Christ you are counted righteous by faith even though you do not obtain perfection.

b. Observe how Christ frees us.

1) He forgives us of sin.

2) He takes away the dominion of the law.

3) He gives us a motive for living righteously.

a) It is not a terror of the law, but love.

b) It is a spontaneous devotion.

3. The word *redeem* and the word *ransom* are used frequently by Paul.

a. "Give his life a ransom." Matt. 20:28

b. "Life a ransom for many." I Tim. 2:6

c. "Ye were bought . . ." I Cor. 6:20 & 7:23

d. "That he might redeem us . . ." Titus 2:14

**having become a curse for us**

1. I believe that Jerome says this verse can not refer to Jesus, but I believe if Jerome belives that, he must not refer to this verse.

2. Paul is not saying that Christ was guilty but that it was for our behalf.

a. The sentence of death has been pronounced upon a sinful world, but Christ took the penalty upon Himself.

b. On February. 9, 1951, television showed a German being released from prison after having served for his father who was condemned as a war criminal.

c. The Scriptures teach that Christ died for us.

1) Isaiah 53:12 "He bare the sins of many."

2) Cf. I Cor. 15:3

3. An extreme position teaches that Christ actually became sin.

a. When He became a curse:

1) He became Peter the liar.

2) He became Paul the persecutor.

3) He became David the adulterer.

4) He became Noah the drunkard.

5) He became Adam the disobedient.

b. II Cor. 5:21 is quoted as proof text: "he made to be sin . . . that we might become the righteousness of God."

4. To ascribe all the sin of man to Christ to make him guilty is not what Paul is teaching.

a. A person who substitutes for another serves as though he were guilty.

b. The result is the same as though he had sinned.

The following is a special outline of the subject, "Curse for us."

A. We best understand this from the Old Testament.

1. Curse has in it the idea of atonement for our sins.

2. Whatever was offered as an atonement for sin was considered as bearing the punishment due to sin.

3. Whoever was hanged was cursed of God and was not to hang over night but to be buried at once to get it out of sight. Deut. 21:22-23

B. The Prophets picture Him as a curse.

1. "Jehovah hath laid on him the iniquity of us all." Isaiah 53:6

2. "Behold, the Lamb of God, that taketh away the sin of the world!" John 1:29

C. Christ became a successful curse.

1. "Triumphing over them." Colossians 2:15

2. "Condemned sin in the flesh." Romans 8:3

D. The scope of Christ as a curse.

1. Christ's cross delivers from the penalty of sin.

2. Christ at God's right hand delivers from the power of sin.

3. Christ at His coming will deliver from the presence of sin.

Observe that everything that Christ did was for us!

### for it is written, Cursed is every one that hangeth on a tree

1. This is a quote from Deut. 21:22-23

2. Ordinarily we say stoning was the Jewish method of capitol punishment and hanging on a cross was the Roman method.

a. Thus Jesus was put to death by the Roman method.

b. It was of course by Jewish request.

3. The following is a history of hanging:

a. The Egyptians practised this before the Romans.

1) "Pharaoh . . . shall hang thee on a tree." Gen. 40:19

2) "But he hanged the chief baker." Gen. 40:22

3) "... him he hanged." Gen. 41:13

b. The Philistines used the method.

1) "where the Philistines had hanged them." II Sam. 21:12

c. The Babylonians used it before the Romans.

1) "To hang Moredcai on the gallows ..." Esther 6:4

2) "The gallows fifty cubits high ..." Esther 7:9

3) "him they have hanged upon the gallows." Esther 8:7

4) "They hanged Haman's ten sons." Esther 9:14

d. It was a Jewish method likewise.

1) "... and thou hang him on a tree ..." Deut. 21:22-23

2) "hanged on a tree." Joshua 8:29

3) "hanged them on five trees." Joshua 10:26

4) II Sam. 4:12 — (The slayers of Ishbosheth — David hanged)

5) "let him be lifted up and fastened thereon (a beam)" Ezra 6:11

6) "Judas hanged himself." Matt. 22:5

e. Jesus was spoken of as hanging on a tree.

1) "Jesus, whom ye slew, hanging him on a tree." Acts 5:30

2) "Whom also they slew, hanging him on a tree." Acts 10:39

4. The conclusion of Paul's argument.

a. The law brought a curse upon all men.

b. Christ took the curse upon Himself.

c. Now in Christ we are free, saved, redeemed; why go back to the curse?

## Comment 3:14

**that upon the Gentiles might come the blessing of Abraham.**

1. The promise was, "In thee shall all the families of the earth be blessed." Gen. 12:3

2. To become a blessing to all, Christ had to become a curse for all.

**that we might receive the promise of the Spirit.**

1. This may refer to the following relationships:

a. "the spirit of adoption." Rom. 8:15

b. "the gift of the Spirit." Acts 2:38

c. "he shall give another comforter." John 14:16

d. "if I go, I will send him (the comforter) unto you." John 16:7

2. Does he mean that we might received the Spirit or the promise of the Spirit?

a. Many commentators ignore this question as though it is not present.

b. It is likely the promise of the spiritual blessings is referred to.

3. This promise is not stated explicitly to Abraham but implied. Gen. 22:17-18

4. It is expressly mentioned by the prophets.

a. "I will pour my Spirit upon thy seed . . ." Isaiah 44:3

b. "I have poured out my Spirit." Ezek. 39:29

c. "I will pour out my Spirit upon all Flesh . . ." Joel 2:28

### through faith

1. Remember, O foolish Galatians, it is obtained through faith in Christ.

2. Faith in Christ would not only save them for eternity but from foolishness.

## Study Questions 3:13-14

299. Were all men under the curse of the law, or just the Hebrews?

300. Is this verse aplicable to us, if he is speaking of the law of Moses?

301. Who all is meant by the word "us"?

302. What enables us to escape the curse?

303. Does this mean that we live Christ's way perfectly although we could not live perfectly in accord with the simple ten commandments?

304. How then does God consider us righteous?

305. Define the words "redeem" and "ransom".

306. Why would Galatians go back to the thing that they were redeemed from?

307. What did Christ become for us, as expressed in this verse?

308. Did Christ become a curse, actually?

309. Was all the sin of the world laid upon Christ? Cf. Isaiah 53:12; II Cor. 5:21

310. Did Christ serve as the sacrifice as though he were guilty?

311. Is it possible for one person to be guilty in place of another?

312. Is assuming one's punishment the same as assuming one's guilt?

313. Is the "how Christ did it" as important as the fact of it?

314. Was Christ a successful curse for us?

315. Name three areas in which Christ was a successful curse as indicated under "scope".

316. What text is quoted by Paul to back up his teaching concerning a curse?
317. Why would Moses refer to "hanging" when the common Jewish method of punishment was stoning?
318. Give evidence that Jews were also hanged.
319. Does Paul teach here that the curse was for Jews only?
320. Did Christ become a curse for all in order to be a blessing for all men?
321. Does he teach that the curse also brought the Spirit?
322. Was the Spirit promised to Abraham?
323. Did the prophets foretell the Spirit?
324. How is the Spirit obtained — by law or by faith?
325. Why would men seek the law, when it cannot produce the Spirit?

## B. SUPERIORITY OF THE GOSPEL TO THE LAW. 3:15-29

1. Illustrated and proved by the covenant with Abraham. 3:15-18

### Text 3:15-18

**15 Brethren, I speak after the manner of men: Though it be but a man's covenant, yet when it hath been confirmed, no one maketh it void, or addeth thereto.   16 Now to Abraham were the promises spoken, and to his seed. He saith not, And to seeds, as of many; but as of one, And to thy seed, which is Christ.   17 Now this I say: A covenant confirmed beforehand by God, the law, which came four hundred and thirty years after, doth not disannul, so as to make the promise of none effect.   18 For if the inheritance is of the law, it is no more of promise: but God hath granted it to Abraham by promise.**

### Paraphrase

15 Brethren, in confuting those who affirm that the blessing of the nations in Abraham, and in his seed, is to be accomplished by their conversion to Judaism, I speak according to the practice of men: No one setteth aside or altereth a ratified covenant, though it but the covenant of a man.

16 Now, to Abraham were the promises made, that in him all the families of the earth shall be blessed; and to his seed, that in it likewise all nations, the Jews not excepted, shall be blessed. God does not say, And in seeds, as speaking concerning many, but as speaking concerning one person he saith, And in thy seed the nations are to be blessed; not through the whole of Abraham's seed, but through one of them only, who is Christ.

17 Wherefore, this I affirm, that the covenant with Abraham, which was anciently ratified by God with an oath, concerning the blessing of the nations in Christ, the law, which was made four hundred and thirty years after, neither with the consent of Abraham, nor of his seed Christ, but of the Jews only, cannot annul, so as to abolish the promise, by introducing a different method of blessing the nations, namely, by the works of the law of Moses.

18 Besides, if the inheritance even of the earthly country be obtained by works of law, it is no longer bestowed by promise as a free gift. Yet Moses expressly declares, that God bestowed the inheritance of Canaan as a free gift on Abraham by promise.

## Comment 3:15

**no one maketh it void, or addeth thereto.**

1. Civil law prohibits tampering, Paul illustrates.
2. Will men dare to observe man's law so carefully, then alter God's?
a. Who would dare to set aside the laws of the Masonic order?
b. Yet men want to add to and take away from God's law.

## Comment 3:16

**To Abraham were the promises spoken, and to his seed**

1. A testament is not a law, but an inheritance.
2. Heirs do not look for laws and assessments when they open a last will, they look for grants and favors.
3. The testament to Abraham contained promises of great spiritual blessing.

**He saith not, And to seeds, as of many: but as of one**

1. The promises were made in view of Christ — one seed.
a. "The gift by the grace of the one man, Jesus Christ, did abound unto the many." Romans 5:15
b. One seed is able to bless all of the seed of Abraham.
2. It is actually two seeds in thought.
a. The physical seed would bring Jesus.
b. The spiritual seed would be Abraham by faith.
c. The Jews argue that seed is a collective noun and refers to many.
d. Paul says it can mean one, and that one is Christ.

## Comment 3:17

### a covenant confirmed beforehand

1. The covenant is made in Gen., chap. 12 and confirmed in chap. 16 and 17.
2. The covenant is confirmed in Gen. 22.
a. "By myself have I sworn saith Jehovah," vs. 16
b. God confirms by swearing by Himself.
c. How many years between Gen. 12 and Gen. 22:16?
1) Abraham departs from Haran — journeys through Canaan — is driven by famine into Egypt — returns from Egypt — battles the Kings — sees the destruction of Sodom — Isaac is born.
2) This accounts for at least 25-40 years.
3. Perhaps there was some other confirmation with Jacob — which would be about 215 years later. See Gen. 28:4

### the law, which came four hundred and thirty years after.

1. This 430 years is a problem of chronology.
a. It is the number given in the Septuagint, and for agrumentative purposes is sufficiently correct as a round number.
b. Perhaps some other confirmation than the one Abraham provides, is the date of reckoning.
2. The time from Abraham is accounted as follows:
a. The promise is made in Gen. 12:3, when Abraham was 75.
b. From the promise to the birth of Isaac was 25 years, when Abraham was 100. Gen. 21:5
c. The birth of Isaac to the birth of Jacob was 60 years. Gen. 25:26
d. From Jacob's birth to the descent to Egypt was 130 years.
e. This would leave 250 years that the Jews were in Egypt.
f. This conflicts seemingly with Exodus 12:40.
1) "Now the time that the children of Israel dwelt in Egypt was four hundred and thirty years."
2) The King James Version says, "Now the sojourning of the children of Israel, who dwelt in Egypt, was four hundred and thirty years."
3. Paul quoted from the Septuagint Version.
4. The Hebrew copies make the sojourn in Egypt 430 years, thus the promise to Abraham 215 years earlier than Jacob's entrance would be 645 which strengthens Paul's argument even more.

**doth not disannul, so as to make the promise of none effect**

1. Evidently the Jewish argument was that the law was given because God was not satisfied with the former.
2. Abraham was never justified by the law, for the law was not in effect for 430 years — possibly 645.
3. If God had meant for us to be justified by law, He would have given it perhaps 430 years before the promise.

## Comment 3:18

**if the inheritance is of the law, it is no more of promise**

1. What God has promised He can not take back from faithful Abraham.
2. An inheritance does not come from two parties.
a. If it came by law — it couldn't come by promise.
b. It came by promise, so law is ruled out.

## Study Questions 3:15-18

326. Why would an inspired apostle speak after the manner of men?
327. What was Paul's illustration?
328. Why do men enforce civil law so carefully yet change God's so thoroughly and feel so lightly about it?
329. What have men added to God's law today?
330. Name the objects of worship today, not taught in the N.T.
331. Does the Scripture warn against adding and taking away?
332. Who was included in Abrahamic promise?
333. Name the phases of the promise?
334. Why is seed in the singular?
335. Whom does the seed refer to?
336. Are we then to be considered seed of Christ?
337. Compare Isaiah 53 to discover if Jesus has seed.
338. What is the covenant referred to?
339. When was the covenant made?
340. When was it confirmed?
341. How was it confirmed?
342. What did this confirmation preceed and why is this important?
343. Was the confirmation ever repeated?
344. If Abraham could be justified before the law — then is it possible for God to justify us today after the law?

345. How is the inheritance given?
346. How faithful is the promise?
347. Was the promise made void by law, since the law came later?

2. Superiority of the Gospel to the Law seen in that the law was a temporary arrangement.  3:19-29

## Text 3:19-20

**19 What then is the law? It was added because of transgressions, till the seed should come to whom the promise hath been made; and it was ordained through angels by the hand of a mediator. 20 Now a mediator is not a mediator of one; but God is one.**

## Paraphrase

19 But if the inheritance was not by the law, but by the promise as a free gift, Why was the law added after the promise? It was added on account of restraining transgressions; and was to continue till the seed should come to whom it was promised, that all nations should be blessed in him; being spoken by angels, who put it in the hand of Moses, as a mediator between God and the people.

20 The giving of the law by a mediator, shewed the Israelites that God was displeased with them; because a mediator is not employed between parties who are in friendship: But God is in friendship only with the righteous.

## Comment 3:19

**What then is the law?**

1. If it does not annul the promise and if it can not confer salvation, why did God send it?
a. Paul states it was added because of transgression.
b. Further, it was only temporary.
c. It was ordained at the hands of angels through a mediator.
d. The law served a very important purpose as a tutor. Gal. 3:14
2. Luther answers like this:
a. That there might be a people of God rigidly controlled out of which could come Jesus Christ.
b. That a people burdened by many laws might sigh and long for a redeemer.
c. The ceremonies foreshadowed Christ.

d. Therefore, the law was meant to confirm the promise until the fulness of time should come.

### It was added because of transgressions

1. It was added to show man's sinfulness and his need of the mercy of God.
2. Men would know sin only in a general way without law.
3. "For until the law sin was in the world; but sin is not imputed when there is no law." Rom. 5:13
4. "I had not known sin, except through the law." Rom. 7:7
5. "For through the law cometh the knowledge of sin." Rom. 3:20

### till the seed should come

1. We have at least a two-fold purpose of the law.
a. One is civil.
1) Law was given to restrain sin.
2) Law seeks to preserve the good.
b. The other is spiritual.
1) The law led us to grace — to Jesus.
2. This gives us the limitation.
a. When God said "forever" He meant it to be until He sent Christ.
1) "It shall be a statute for ever throughout their generations on the behalf of the children of Israel. Exodus 27:21
2) "And this day shall be unto you for a memorial, and ye shall keep it a feast to Jehovah: (passover) throughout your generations, ye shall keep it a feast by an ordinance forever." Exodus 12:14

### to whom the promise hath been made

1. Was the promise made to Jesus? No.
2. "To whom" refers to the descendants of Abraham.

### it was ordained through angels

1. What is "it"?
a. The promise? No.
b. The law. Yes.
c. It was not given by divine lips as to Abraham directly.
d. It was given by angels
1) "He shined forth from mount Paran and he came from the ten thousand of holy ones: at his right hand was a fiery law for them." Deut. 33:2

2) "For if the word spoken through angels proved steadfast, and every transgression and disobedience received a just recompence of reward" Heb. 2:2

3) "The chariots of God are twenty thousand, even thousands upon thousands: The Lord is among them, as in Sinai, in the sanctuary." Psalm 68:17

4) "The law as it was ordained by angels." Acts 7:53

e. This, of course, is not as great as swearing by Himself.
1) It was given in a different way in a different manner.
2) There was no mediator between God and Abraham.
f. Note the limiation of the mediator.
1) Moses was only a mediator between God and Israel, not between God and Spiritual Israel.
2) Thus a promise to include everyone could not be altered by a covenant such as the one Moses gave.
2. "Ordained" simply means that angels mediated it and it was no less divine. Cf. Heb. 2:2, Acts 7:38,53

**by the hand of the mediator**

1. Moses was the mediator.
"I stood between Jehovah and you at that time, to show you the word of Jehovah: for ye were afraid because of the fire, and went not up into the mount." Deut. 5:5
2. There was no mediator between Abraham and God: He acted singularly.

## Comment 3:20

**now a mediator is not a mediator of one**

1. The Catholic Bible says, "Now there is no intermediary where there is only one."
2. This verse has many ideas: first, what is a mediator?
a. A mediator signifies a middle person: There must necessarily be two parties.
1) He acts in reference to both.
2) He is supposed to have the interests of both equally at heart.
b. Though Moses was a mediator between God and its one seed which is to come;
1) He was the mediator of one part of Abraham's seed, but not the mediator of the other seed.
2) The mediator of the Gentiles is Christ.

**God is one**

1. "God is one, and he shall justify the circumcision by faith, and the uncircumcision through faith." Romans 3:30
a. You can't be a mediator of God only — for God is one.
b. God does not offend any one, therefore He needs no mediator.
2. Hear O Israel: Jehovah our God is one Jehovah. Deut. 6:4
a. The Hebrew word for one is *Ethod.*
1) It means to unite.
2) It means a compound unity.
b. The Scriptures offer the following illustrations:
1) One day — combining light and dark. Gen. 1:5
2) One flesh — made two. Gen. 2:2-24
3) One tribe — one of 12. Gen. 49:16
4) One of a cluster. Numbers 13:23
c. It is seen also in the use of language.
1) Motto of U.S. *E Pluribus Unum* a unity of many — one composed of many.

## Study Questions 3:19-20

348. Are you able to answer Paul's question?
349. Why was the law added?
350. If it can't offer salvation and did not change the promise, then why was it given?
351. To what was it added?
352. How long was the law to last?
353. Did not God say that the Jews were to keep the law forever?
354. Who is refered to by the expression "To whom the promise hath been made"?
355. Was the promise ordained?
356. What does "it" refer to?
357. How was it by angels?
358. Were angels involved in the giving of the promise?
359. Define "mediator."
360. Why did God give the law by a mediator?
361. Does this indicate anything, the fact that the law was given by a mediator, while the promise was not.
362. How many parties are involved when a mediator is used?
363. Was the mediator of Moses limited in his scope?
364. Why does he say "God is one" in this connection?
365. Is it possible for God, the Son, and the Holy Spirit, to be one?
366. Do we use the word "one" to include many?

## Text 3:21,22

**21 Is the law then against the promises of God? God forbid: for if there had been a law given which could make alive, verily righteousness would have been of the law. 22 But the scripture shut up all things under sin, that the promise by faith in Jesus Christ might be given to them that believe.**

### Paraphrase

21 Is not the law, then, which subjects men to the curse for their sins, contrary to the promises of God, wherein he declares that he will justify them by faith? By no means. The law, by subjecting men to the curse, without giving them the least hope of mercy, obliges them to flee to the promises for justification. For if there had been a law given, which was able to make sinners alive, either from the spiritual death under which they were lying, or from the temporal death to which they were condemned for their sins, certainly justification would have been obtained by that law.

22 But, so far is this from being the case, that the scripture hath shut up together all, as condemned to death on account of sin (that is, hath declared that they are so shut up) that the promise of justification made known by the gospel of Jesus Christ might be given to them who believe.

### Comment 3:21

**Is the law then against the promises of God?**

1. No — God can not act in a contrary way.
2. The law is not a competitor nor in opposition.

**if there had been a law given which could make alive**

1. If it could give life, it would be a rival to the gospel.
2. Some divide the law into a ceremonial part and a moral part.
3. Still, the Word says there is no law able — not one.

### Comment 3:22

**but the Scripture shut up all things under sin**

1. All the prophets declared men were sinners.
a. The O. T. prophets did not foretell alone, but preached against sin.
b. In the N. T. John the Baptist preached vigorously about sin to the Jews.

91

1) The Jews considered themselves righteous and the Gentiles sinners.
2) Jesus' parable of the good Samaritan rather reversed the picture as did the story of the Publican.
2. The law prescribed means of taking care of sins.
3. Men were locked in sin until such a time as they could be released, according to Paul.
a. There is a graphic picture of men in sin in Romans 3:19-20
b. "For God hath shut up all unto disobedience, that he might have mercy upon all." Romans 11:32

**the promise by faith in Jesus Christ might be given to them that believe**
1. All were prisoners of hope.
2. Thus the law was not against the Gospel, but helped men to see the blessedness of the Gospel.

### Study Questions 3:21,22
367. Is God acting contrary to himself in giving the law?
368. Is the law in competition to the promise?
369. If the law could give life, would it be a rival to the promise?
370. Is the law divided by Paul into Moral law and Ceremonial law?
371. What is meant by "the scriptures shut up"?
372. Tell what is included in "all things."
373. How long were things locked up?
374. What could do the releasing?
375. Why did men need to be shut up in order to be prisoners of hope?

### Text 3:23-25
**23 But before faith came, we were kept in ward under the law, shut up unto the faith which should afterwards be revealed. 24 So that the law is become our tutor to bring us unto Christ, that we might be justified by faith. 25 But now that faith is come, we are no longer under a tutor.**

### Paraphrase
23 Wherefore, before the gospel was published, we were kept in durance under law—the law of nature and of Moses; shut up together as criminals whom these laws had condemned, to make us embrace the law of faith which should afterwards be revealed.

24 So that the law of nature and of Moses, by making us sensible of the impossibility of being meritoriously justified by works, hath in all ages been our pedagogue to bring us to Christ, that we might be justified by faith gratuitously.

25 But the law of faith being promulgated, we in that dispensation are no longer under the pedagogue. There is no occasion for the law as a pedagogue to bring us to Christ.

### Comment 3:23

**But before faith came we were kept in ward under the law**

1. That is, before faith in Jesus, before the gospel was published.
2. The law serves as a prison, keeping men from evil deeds and enforcing an outward behaviour.

**shut up unto the faith which should afterwards be revealed**

1. Law existed until the day of faith.
a. John declared a new lamb to take away sin. Jn. 1:29
b. Jesus preached the new birth. Jn. 3:3
c. John declared his purpose in writing. Jn. 20:30-31
d. At Pentecost a new Spirit was declared. Acts 2:38
e. The apostles declared a new Gospel. I Cor. 15:1-5
2. A new revelation eliminates the authority of the old.

### Comment 3:24

**is become our tutor**

1. McGarvey states that most families had a slave, who served as a tutor or who took the child to the teacher. He had charge of him from childhood to manhood to shield and protect him.
2. He affirms that the law was such a tutor to bring those under its care to a state of development fit for society and fellowship of Christ, the spiritual father.

**that we might be justified by faith**

1. Not justified by the work of the law, but faith.
2. This phrase is repeated much in the Scriptures but many do not believe the truthfulness of it.
3. He does not say "faith alone." This is not all of it.

### Comment 3:25

**we are no longer under a tutor.**

1. The tutor authority ceased with the day of Pentecost when the gospel was preached.
2. This is emphasized in many passages.

a. "Having abolished . . . the law of commandments." Eph.
2:14-15

b. Having blotted out the bond written in ordinances . . . nailing
it to the cross." Col. 2:14

3. The tutor was the law and Paul says that we are not under it.
The Christian is strictly a new covenant person.

## Study Questions 3:23-25

376. What faith is referred to here?
377. How was man inward?
378. Under what sentence did man live inward?
379. Define the day of faith.
380. What purpose did the law serve as stated in this verse?
381. How long was the law a tutor?
382. Do we need a tutor when we learn from Christ?
383. Does he say that "faith only" will justify?
384. It is well to name the various elements stated in the word
of God that do justify.
385. Does he teach that Christ is sufficient?
386. If Christ is sufficient, then are works of the law insufficient?
387. Why do men hold to the law, a tutor, when Paul says we
are not under it?

## Text 3:26-29

**26 For ye are all sons of God, through faith, in Christ Jesus.
27 For as many of you as were baptized into Christ did put on
Christ.  28 There can be neither Jew nor Greek, there can be
neither bond nor free, there can be no male and female; for ye
all are one man in Christ Jesus.  29 And if ye are Christ's, then
are ye Abraham's seed heirs according to promise.**

## Paraphrase

26 It is not necessary to your being the sons of God, and heirs
of the promise, that ye be under the law: For ye are all the sons
of God, through your believing the gospel published by Christ
Jesus.

27 Besides, as many of you as have been baptized into Christ,
have thereby professed that ye have put on the very temper and
virtues of Christ, God's greatest Son; and having so done, ye are
really, not nominally, the sons of God, and are greatly beloved
of your Father.

28 In Christ Jesus there is no distinction of persons, as under the law: under the gospel, no Jew is superior to a Greek, neither are slaves inferior to free men; nor are males preferred to females; for ye are all one, in respect of dignity and privileges, under the gospel dispensation.

29 And if ye be Christ's brethren by possessing his temper of mind, certainly ye are Abraham's seed, more really than those Jews who are related to him only by natural descent, and heirs of the heavenly country according to God's promise to Abraham.

## Comment 3:26

### ye are all sons of God, through faith, in Jesus Christ

1. You can be a child of God without Jewish blood or submitting to a Jewish rite.
2. The condition of sonship.
a. Relationship.
b. Adoption.
c. Liberty.
3. The origin of sonship.
a. Through faith.
b. Through union with Christ by baptism.
4. The consequences of sonship.
a. Universal brotherhood:  social and racial differences cease.
b. Inheritance or ancient promises.

## Comment 3:27

### as were baptized into Christ

(Cath.— who have been baptized into Christ)
1. How do we get into Christ?  "Baptized into."
2. The verb tense is past, completed action.
3. There are two classes of prepositions.
a. One means motion.
b. One means rest.
c. The preposition here is motion. We have moved into Christ where there is no condemnation. "There is therefore now no condemnation . . ." Rom. 8:1

### did put on Christ

1. This means to put on or to be clothed with one.
a. It means to assume the character of the one.
b. The Christian is to assume the character of Christ.

2. The old man must be put off first.

a. "our old man was crucified" Romans 6:1

b. "That ye put away, as concerning your former manner of life, the old man, that wareth corrupt after the lusts of deceit." Eph. 4:22

c. "But put ye on the Lord Jesus Christ, and make not provision for the flesh, to fulfill the lusts thereof." Romans 13:14

3. "He clothes us with righteousness of Christ by means of baptism." Luther

## Comment 3:28

**for ye are all one man in Christ Jesus.**

1. There can be no difference if faith is the one way.

2. Circumstances of birth or personal worth, mean nothing.

3. We become in the individual sense, sons of God; but distinctions are lost in the collective sense, so that race, gender, and castes, are gone.

a. It would be strange to have one faith, one Lord and one baptism, and two ranks of people.

b. This oneness will bring the union of God's people.

c. The Word does not speak of union of denominations, but oneness in Christ.

## Comment 3:29

**if ye be Christs**

1. Two important things hinge on this.

a. We are Abraham's seed.

b. We are heirs.

2. The relationship to the inheritance hinges on our relationship to Christ.

## Study Questions 3:26-29

388. How inclusive is the word "all?"

389. Are we included without Jewish blood?

390. Are we excluded without Jewish rites?

391. On what does sonship depend?

392. Define baptism.

393. Is this water or spirit baptism?

394. How do we get into Christ?

395. Does this mean that we change our abode when we come into Christ?

96

396. Is a person in Christ without baptism?
397. Is a man a brother in Christ, who professes Christianity and yet who will not be baptized?
398. Is a man a brother if he accepts a substitute baptism?
399. What is meant by putting on Christ?
400. Do you have to put something off in order to put on Christ?
401. What will a person be like if he has Christ on him?
402. Does this verse teach that we are clothed with Christ's righteousness by means of baptism?
403. Is baptism work or faith?
404. Do we submit to baptism by faith or do we do it as work?
405. What barriers are erased by baptism into Christ?
406. Can we have ranks of people with one faith and one baptism?
407. What does this verse do to the color line?
408. Does this verse destroy denominational lines?
409. In what relationship are we to Abraham?
410. How does this relationship affect the promise?
411. What do we belong to in order to be entitled to the promise?
412. How big is the word "if" in this verse?

## Questions on Galatians, Chapter Three
### True - False

_____ 1. Christ ransomed us from the Law's curse by taking our curse upon himself.

_____ 2. The law is a schoolmaster to bring men to Christ.

_____ 3. Because our faith is never complete men are always under the schoolmaster or tutor.

_____ 4. Baptism into Christ is a "putting on" of the law.

_____ 5. All men are one in Christ, except those of different color.

_____ 6. If we belong to Christ, then we are truly descendents of Abraham and his heirs under the promise.

_____ 7. The law was given shortly after Abraham was justified by faith.

_____ 8. The law was added because of transgressions.

_____ 9. All who rely on works of the law are under a curse.

_____10. The law of Moses annulled any covenant previously made by God.

_____11. Paul maintained that obedience is better than sacrifice.

_____12. The Spirit was given to the Galatians through the working of the law.

_____13. Some stern things are said to the Galatians in this chapter.

_____14. Paul laid all the blame on the Galatians.

_____15. Paul tells the Galatians that they were foolish.

_____16. When we have had faith, we have put on Christ according to Gal. 3:27.

_____17. If we are Christ's we may be considered as Abraham's seed. vs. 29

_____18. The promise to Abraham was at least 430 years before the Israelites were at Sinai.

_____19. As many as are of the works of the law are under a curse.

_____20. An argument of Paul's in Galatians is that the law should not be obeyed because it was against the promises of God.

**Completion:**

1. What then is the law? It was _____ because of transgression.

2. O _____ Galatians who did betwitch you?

3. Even as Abraham believed God, and it was reckoned unto him for _____.

4. For it is written, cursed is everyone that hangeth on a _____.

5. Now that faith is come, we are no longer under a _____.

6. The law which came _____ years after, doth not disannul, so as to make the promise of none effect.

## C. ILLUSTRATION AS TO WHY THE LAW PRECEDED AND MUST GIVE WAY TO THE GOSPEL. 4:1-31

1. Childhood and manhood. 4:1-11

### Text 4:1-4

**1 But I say that so long as the heir is a child, he differeth nothing from a bondservant though he is lord of all; 2 but is under guardians and stewards until the day appointed of the father.**

**3 So we also, when we were children, were held in bondage under the rudiments of the world:   4 but when the fulness of the time came, God sent forth his Son, born of a woman, born under the law,**

### Paraphrase

1 Now if ye ask, why the gospel dispensation was not introduced immediately after the fall? and why the heirs, during so many ages, were left to the guidance of the laws of nature and

of Moses? I answer, As long as the heir is a child, he differeth nothing from a bond-man, although by right of inheritance he be proprietor of the whole estate:

2 For he is put under instructors who teach him, and stewards who manage his estate, and supply him with necessaries, until the time before appointed of his father, for giving him the possession of his inheritance, arriveth.

3 So also we, the heirs of the promises, whilst we were children, were not put in possession of the promises, by the introduction of the gospel dispensation, immediately after the fall, but, to fit us for that dispensation, were placed in bondage under the elements of the world.

4 But when the time, before appointed of the Father for putting the heirs in possession of the promises, by introducing the gospel dispensation, was fully come, God sent forth, from heaven into our world, his Son, born of a woman, and born under the law;

## Comment 4:1

**so long as the heir is a child**

1. This is to show why the bondage of the law preceded the liberty of the gospel.
2. Childhood is for a period of development. And in the ancient household he was little more than a slave.
3. Faith in Christ makes man a mature heir.

## Comment 4:2

**but is under guardians and stewards**

1. He must needs be under constant care — otherwise he would be in constant danger of losing the inheritance.
2. He is not able to order his own affairs, but is just like a servant.
a. Observe how God had to deal with the Hebrews, then this verse.
b. Foolish Galatians are acting as though they are going back to this state.

**until the day**

1. A specified time of the father's choosing.
2. The day that is appropriate — a "full day" or fulness of time.

**appointed by the Father**

1. People in society have a day for their daughter's debut.
2. A father in business has a day when he retires and turns over all to his son.

## Comment 4:3

**we were children**

1. Law is childhood stage — what a time God has had with His infants.
2. Paul warns Christians about infancy.
a. ". . . I fed you with milk . . ." I Cor. 3:2
b. ". . . Such as have need of milk . . ." Heb. 5:12

**held in bondage**

1. You do not allow children very much freedom.
a. You want them to grow.
b. You want to teach them.
2. The day comes when you let them go in confidence.
3. God gives Christians freedom.
a. They have the Spirit to guide them.
b. The only freedom is in Christ, but it is not a license to do evil.

**under the rudiments**

1. Paul may mean — The law is earthly.
a. It restrains from evil, but does not deliver from sin.
b. It does not justify. You do not earn eternal life just because you do not kill, commit adultery, etc.
2. Luther says Paul is referring principally to the ceremonial law which dealt with external matters as meat, drink, dress, places, times, feasts, cleansings, sacrifices, etc.

## Comment 4:4

**but when the fulness of time came**

1. The Greek language had spread so that it was practically universal.
2. Roman government had brought some good influences.
a. Roman roads — making traveling safe.
b. Roman law and order.
3. There had been four hundred years of silence allowing mankind to find out that he could not do without God.
a. People were deteriorating in their lusts. Romans 1:20
4. When the time came for the termination of a period of tutorship then God took steps for the liberation of all mankind.

**God sent forth his Son**

1. This is God's supreme effort.
2. Jesus sets forth this event in the parable of the vineyard. Matt. 21:33-39

3. Prophets were sent and God worked hard to display His love but the gift of His Son makes other attempts seem small.

### born of a woman

1. Christ's birth was of a virgin according to prophecy and the Gospels.
2. Why is not the virgin birth taught here?
a. Some say it is taught when he says "born of a woman!" otherwise, he would have said, "born of a man," or "man and woman."
b. The human side of Jesus is tremendously important.
1) We know He knows our weaknesses, for He lived as we.
2) See Heb. 4:15

### born under the law

1. He voluntarily placed Himself under the law and permitted it to have dominion over Him.
a. Actually the law had no dominion over him.
1) "Who did no sin, neither was guile found in his mouth." I Peter 2:22
b. Yet the law treated this innocent, just, and blessed lamb of God as cruelly as any.
c. He did not fulfill any one or two easy requirements of the law, but endured all.
2. The Jews accused him of breaking the law, but He only broke their traditions.

## Study Questions 4:1-4

413. What is Paul's argument in this verse?
414. Why is a child like a bondservant?
415. How is the child different?
416. What is the childhood period for?
417. Describe what is involved under guardianship.
418. Should we be proud and haughty, while we are children expecting to be heirs?
419. Do we have special days for children?
420. Do earthly fathers appoint days for their children?
421. Compare this idea with fullness of time expressed in verse 4.
422. Does Paul mean that the law was a childhood age?
423. Did God have an easy time with his children during Moses' day?

424. Do we allow children very much freedom?

425. Is Paul saying that the law was a period of bondage?

426. Is freedom a period of license?

427. What is meant by rudiments?

428. Does he mean that the law is a rudiment?

429. Is Paul teaching that while we are in bondage to the law, we are under the rudiments of the world?

430. How could a law of God be considered a rudiment of the world?

431. Could Luther be right in dividing the law into a ceremonial law suggesting that these things are meant by rudiments?

432. What is meant by "fulness of time?"

433. In what way was it a full time?

434. Does it refer to the termination of a period of tutorship?

435. What great event took place in this full time?

436. Is this verse avoiding the virgin birth?

437. Why is Paul emphasizing the human side of Christ?

438. If Christ was born under the law, then was He automatically under the curse?

439. Since Christ was sinless, was He not under the law?

440. If Jews accused Christ of breaking the law and they were the ones to enforce the law, was He under a curse?

## Text 4:5-7

**5 that he might redeem them that were under the law, that we might receive the adoption of sons. 6 And because ye are sons, God sent forth the Spirit of his Son into our hearts, crying, Abba, Father. 7 So that thou art no longer a bondservant, but a son; and if a son, then an heir through God.**

## Paraphrase

5 That, by his obedience unto death, he might buy off Jews and Gentiles who were under law, that we might receive the adoption of sons; that we Gentiles might be made the people of God, and receive the blessings belonging to the people of God, by being introduced into the gospel church.

6 And because ye believing Jews and Gentiles are sons, God hath sent forth the Spirit of his Son into your hearts, by whose gifts, being assured that ye are God's sons, ye can address him in prayer with confidence, calling him, each in your own language, Abba, Father.

7 So that thou who possessest the gifts of the Spirit art no more a bond-man, under law as a rule of justification, and driven to obey by the fear of punishment; but a son actuated by love: and if a son, then an heir of God through Christ.

## Comment 4:5

**that he might redeem**
1. Redeem means to pay down a price for them.
2. Redeem — buying them off from the necessity of observing circumcision, and offering brute sacrifices.
3. This states the result of Jesus' coming.
4. This states a fulfillment of Gen. 22:18 "In thy seed shall all the nations of the earth be blessed."

**that we might receive the adoption of sons**
1. Christ made it possible, but we have a responsibility.
a. "Wherefore Come ye out from among them, and be ye separate, saith the Lord, and touch no unclean thing; and I will receive you, And will be to you a Father and ye shall be to me sons and daughters, saith the Lord Almighty." II Cor. 6:17
b. To be adopted by God is a distinct honor.
c. On earth we do not have the privilege to select our father but we do for eternity.
d. This gives us the right to call God "Father" Cf. 4:6
2. In this relationship we become joint heirs with Jesus Christ Cf. Rom. 8:17

## Comment 4:6

**and because ye are sons**
1. The Spirit was not sent to make us sons, but is sent when we become sons.
2. Sonship comes as a result of the adoption process as a result of faith.
a. "As many as received Him to them He gave the right to become children of God." John 1:12
b. The promise of the Spirit is made to the repentant and obedient ones. Acts 2:38

**God sent forth the Spirit of his Son**
1. The Spirit of slavery to the devil must depart in order for Christ's spirit to come in.

2. The Spirit is the Spirit of Christ.

a. Since Christ through His work has received our adoption as sons, His Spirit can be sent to those who belong to Him.

b. Gal. 3:26 says we are Sons by faith. And 3:27 says by baptism we get into Christ and put Him on.

c. Faith, baptism and the Spirit of Christ, are inseparable.

3. The outpouring of the Spirit belonged to the promised Messiah. Cf. Joel 2:28-29

**into our hearts**

1. Proper faith and baptism must concern the earnest person who desires the spirit of Christ in his heart.

a. What Scriptural Baptism Requires:
Water, Acts 10:47; Acts 8:36-38
Much water, John 3:23
Going to water, Mark 1:9
Going down into water, Acts 8:38
Coming up out of water, Mark 1:10; Acts 8:39
Born of water, John 3:5
Form of burial, Col. 2:12
Form of Resurrection, Romans 6:4
Bodies washed, Heb. 10:22
　　Immersion meets all the requirements of Scriptural baptism, while sprinkling only meets one — water.
　　Why call ye me, Lord, Lord, and do not the things which I say. Luke 6:46. If ye love me, ye will keep my commandments, John 14:15.

b. Results Following Bible Baptism:
Sins remitted  Acts 2:38
Gift of the Holy Ghost  Acts 2:38
In Christ  Gal. 3:27
In the Church  I Cor. 12:13
A good Conscience  I Peter 3:21
A Christian Life  Rom. 6:4
Heaven  Rev. 22:14

2. The heart is the center of ones will and affections and therefore will not have Christ's Spirit until submitted to His will.

**crying, Abba, Father**

1. It is in Christ that we cry to God.
a. We have here an Aramaic and Greek word with the same meaning.
b. They were the two languages in which Christians of that day worshipped God.
c. With the fulfillment of the prophecies (Cf. Isaiah 44:3) concerning the Messiah, men were permitted to call God, Abba.
2. It seems that Jesus originated the use of the word, Abba. Cf. Mark 14:36.
a. Jesus could do this, because of His fellowship with God.
b. We can do it, if we have a proper obedience.
3. This is a unique statement.
a. It fulfills Messianic prophecies. Cf. Jer. 3:19, 31:9; Ps. 89:27.
b. It has four limitations in time.
1) It belongs to the time of the fufillment of the promise.
2) The time of the inheritance.
3) The time of freedom.
4) The time of sonship.
4. Those who go back to the law, depart from this great truth that made this wonderful relationship possible.

## Comment 4:7

**Thou art no longer a bondservant**

1. He who could receive the Spirit and pray "Abba Father" has no reason to go back to bondage.
a. The Chrsitian is a faithful person who has grown up to be an heir.
b. The Christian has been redeemed by Christ and has changed relationship from a child who was a bondservant to a mature person who is an heir.
c. This was the whole purpose of the fulness of time.
2. Two things from which man is free:
a. Power, dominion of sin Cf. Rom. 8:2; 8:13
b. The Mosaic law. Gal. 4:8-10; 3:24

**But a Son**

1. Sons have many advantages.
a. An inheritance. Rom. 8:17
b. freedom Gal. 5:1
c. fellowship with the Father as sons. John 1:11; Cf. I John 1:3,6-7

2. The Christian must appreciate this new relationship and never go back to the world.

a. Like a dog and hog.  II Peter 2:20

b. ". . . whose end is to be burned."  Heb. 6:4

### If a Son then an heir

1. As a member of the family we have a right to the properties.

a. We are baptized in the name of Jesus Christ.

b. This means into the possessions of the one so named — according to some Greek usages in natural life.

2. It is an inheritance of another world where the treasures can not be destroyed — and are eternal.

a. Cf. Jesus' statement Matt. 6:19

b. Cf. Peter's statement I Peter 1:4

c. Cf. Paul's statement Heb. 9:15

### Through God

1. This verse does not eliminate Christ and His part.

2. Divine truth is never expressed fully in one verse in the language of man.

## Study Questions 4:5-7

441. Does this verse answer why Christ was born under the law?

442. If He could redeem Gentiles, who were not under the law of Moses, why could He not redeem the Jews also?

443. What law is referred to here?

444. In what way are we sons according to this verse?

445. Did He send His Spirit to make us sons?

446. Is the Spirit of His Son, the same as the Spirit promised on Pentecost?

447. Does the promise of the Comforter refer to this same Spirit?

448. What is the significance of "into hearts"?

449. What does the word "Abba" mean?

450. Why did Paul use two different languages here?

451. What state did we leave when we accepted Christ?

452. What does a son have that a bondservant does not?

453. Why do men reject the privilege to be an heir and remain in bondage?

454. What all is involved in heirship?

455. Do we have a property right to God's wealth?

## Text 4:8-11

8 Howbeit at that time, not knowing God, ye were in bondage to them that by nature are no gods:   9 but now that ye have come to know God, or rather to be known by God, how turn ye back again to the weak and beggarly rudiments, whereunto ye desire to be in bondage over again?   10 Ye observe days, and months, and season, and years.   11 I am afraid of you, lest by any means I have bestowed labor upon you in vain.

## Paraphrase

8 However, that ye Gentiles may not foolishly renounce your privileges as the sons of God, ye ought to remember what your condition was whilst under the elements of the world, and compare it with your present happy state: That then, indeed, not knowing God, ye served slavishly, beings who are not gods by their own nature, but by human appointment.

9 But now, under the gospel, having acknowledged the true God as your father, (ver. 6) or rather, being acknowledged by him as sons, why, by embracing Judaism, turn ye back again to the unprofitable and low kind of worship formerly practiced by you in your heathenish state, and to which again, ever since your conversion, ye incline to be in bondage?

10 Why do ye carefully observe days, and moons, and seasons, and years? These holidays, though enjoined by Moses are equally ineffectual with the rites of the heathen religions, formerly practiced by you, for procuring the favour of God.

11 Ye are so fond of these weak and poor elements, that I am afraid of you, lest perhaps I have preached in vain among you. For ye do not seem to understand the value the privileges of the gospel.

## Comment 4:8

### Howbeit
1. Means when.
2. A time element is referred to and a condition during that time.

### Not knowing God
1. This verse can be used to imply that the Galatian converts were formerly heathen, which is the preferable view.
2. A second meaning may be found in the fact that the Jews did not know God, even though they worshipped the true God.

a. "It is my Father that glorifieth me; of whom ye say, that he is your God; and ye have not known him: but I know him." John 8:54-55

b. "And these things will they do, because they have not known the Father, nor me." John 16:3

### ye were in bondage to them that by nature are no gods

1. This definitely sounds as though they were heathen.
2. What is the nature of God?
a. A creator and not a creature.
b. A personality, not lifeless material shaped by human hands, which the Galatians no doubt had worshipped.

## Comment 4:9

### now that ye have come to know God

1. How do we know God?
a. By His works — Handiwork. Psalms 19:1
b. By His words — Preaching. I Cor. 1:21
c. By His workman — Jesus revealed. Heb. 1:1-4
1) "The only begotten Son, who is in the bosom of the Father, he hath declared him." John 1:18
2) "He that hath seen me hath seen the Father."
2. Paul also was a workman preaching. John 14:9
a. "I planted, Apollos watered . . ." I Cor. 3:6
b. "That I might not build on another man's foundation." Romans 15:20

### or rather to be known by God

1. This probably means to be approved of God.
2. God does know his own.
a. "Your Father knoweth what things ye have need of." Matt. 6:8
b. "God, who knoweth the heart." Acts 15:8
c. "The Lord knoweth them that are his." II Tim. 2:19
d. "The Lord knoweth how to deliver." II Peter 2:9
e. "Jehovah knoweth the way of the righteous." Psalms 1:6

### How turn ye back again

1. Observe that they once were Christian and were approved of God.
a. People can turn back and be lost
1) "Ye are severed from Christ . . . ye are fallen away from grace." Gal. 5:4

2) "who hindered you . . ." Gal. 5:7

3) "who did bewitch you . . ." Gal. 3:1

4) "Quickly removing" Gal. 1:6

b. Many Scriptures in other places warn about turning back.

1) "Having put his hand to the plow, and looking back." Luke 9:62

2) "Again entangled therein." II Peter 2:20-22

3) "Lest haply we drift away." Heb. 2:1

4) "Falling away." Heb. 3:12

5) "And then fell away, it is impossible to renew them." Heb. 6:6

2. Some religionist formerly argued, "If you get it, you can't lose it; if you lose it, you never had it." But these had it in Galatia.

### To the weak and beggarly rudiments

1. In what way were they weak?

a. Weak — ineffectual rites and ceremonies of Moses.

b. Weak — counteraction to sins.

c. Beggarly element — Too poor to purchase eternal salvation.

d. The weakness of the law: "What the law could not do." Romans 8:3

2. If these are referred to, then they must have been addicted to them at one time for he says "Again."

a. It could be they were heathen who were converted to Judaism, then converted to Christianity.

b. He may be placing all efforts to be righteous by work under the same category whether it be heathen or Jewish.

### rudiments

1. "Rudiments" means unwrought, ignorant, rude, that which is undeveloped.

2. They were rudiments because they belonged to a rudimentary condition.

a. Observe the stages of man's relationship to God.

1) Patriarchal Dispensation.............................................Infancy age.

2) Mosaic dispensation ....................................................Childhood.

3) Christian ......................................................................Manhood.

b. Observe a comparison of the law and the Gospel.

1) Law ...............................................................................Gospel

2) Childhood ....................................................................Manhood

3) Bondage .......................................................................Freedom

4) Inheritance-temporal, now, ........................................Inheritance
                                                                    Spiritual, future.

**Whereunto ye desire to be in bondage over again?**

1. This bondage is to Judaistic teachers.
2. It does not necessarily mean, again to the same thing.
3. They were in bondage in heathenism and were made free and again were going into bondage, this time to false teachers.

**Ye observe days, and months, and seasons, and years.**

1. This is proof of their childhood.
2. The Catholic Bible footnotes this as "Their feasts under the Jewish law."

## Comment 4:10

**Ye observe days**

1. It is not stated whether these were sabbaths and Jewish festivals or ritual days of paganism — maybe both.
a. Col. 2:16 shows it is not a requirement of Christians.
2. Catholics have their days.
a. No meat on Friday — but whiskey can be drunk.
b. Observance is more important than one's life.
c. Saints are worshipped.
d. Festivals are conducted in the name of God.

**And months**

1. Perhaps festivals such as those of tabernacles, dedication, passover, year of Jubilee, etc.
2. Heathen people also have their seasons, believing that astronomical relationships have special significance for human life.

**And seasons**

1. We hear folk talk about Lenten season.
a. Is godliness seasonable?
b. Is self-denial to be periodical?
2. Security is not found in observances.

**And years**

1. Annual atonements, sabbatical years and jubilees are referred to, says Johnson in his notes.
2. Did not Paul observe them? Yes, he did.
a. "Hastening . . . to be at Jerusalem the day of Pentecost." Acts 20:16
b. "But I will tarry at Ephesus until Pentecost." I Cor. 16:8
3. Why did he?

110

a. These were national days. A Jew would remember the pass-over, the giving of the law, etc., as naturally as we remember the Fourth of July.

b. He did not insist upon them as religious rites for Gentiles.

4. The Christian is to live minute by minute and not in relation-ship to man-made observances.

## Comment 4:11

**I am afraid of you, lest by any means I have bestowed labor upon you in vain.**

1. If they were saved — he did not labor in vain — but they had exchanged freedom for bondage, life for death.

a. If once saved always saved be true, then Paul had not labored in vain.

b. Evidently Paul did not teach "Once in grace always in grace," but the exact opposite.

## Study Questions 4:8-11

456. Define the word "howbeit".

457. Judging by the expression "not knowing God" were the Galations formerly heathens or Jehovah worshippers?

458. Did the Jews know God even though they professed to worship Him?

459. To whom were the Galatians in bondage?

460. Does the last expression in the verse suggest strongly that they had been heathen?

461. How did the Galatians come to know God?

462. Do we know God by revelation only?

463. Did God accept the Galatians, according to this verse?

464. Does the scripture offer much assurance that God knows the Christians?

465. Could you turn your back on God as Paul accuses the Galatians?

466. How could they turn from God, who is strong, to weak and beggarly rudiments?

467. List all the expressions in this book that teach the backsliding of the Galatians.

468. Name the verses in the Bible that warn us concerning falling away.

469. In what way were the rudiments weak?

470. Explain how they may be considered beggarly?
471. Were they again in bondage to the same thing?
472. Is bondage to false truth equivalent to being in bondage to false teachers?
473. Were they guilty of strange observances?
474. Do we know if the observances were Jewish or pagan?
475. Are religious festivals generally filled with inconsistencies?
476. Was Paul inconsistent when he went to Jerusalem for their great days such as the Passover?
477. Is it wrong for us to observe our national days?
478. Would it be wrong in binding them upon others as essential for justification?
479. What did Paul mean by his fear?
480. Was his labor in vain, if they were saved in spite of their falling away?
481. What was Paul's labor?

2. Appeal 4:12-20

## Text 4:12-15

**12 I beseech you, brethren, become as I am, for I also am become as ye are. Ye did me no wrong: 13 but ye know that because of an infirmity of the flesh I preached the gospel unto you the first time: 14 and that which was a temptation to you in my flesh ye despised not, nor rejected; but ye received me as an angel of God, even as Christ Jesus. 15 Where then is that gratulation of yourselves? for I bear you witness, that, if possible, ye would have plucked out your eyes and given them to me.**

## Paraphrase 4:12-15

12 Brethren, I pray you to continue in friendship with me; for I am your true friend, having reproved you from love, and not from resentment. For all the time I was with you, ye injured me in nothing.

13 On the contrary, ye behaved towards me with the greatest respect and affection. Ye remember, certainly, that under a bodily infirmity, which might have rendered my labours ineffectual, I preached the gospel to you at first.

14 Yet my bodily infirmity, which was a temptation to me, ye did not ridicule, neither did ye reject me with abhorrence as an

112

imposter, but received me as an angel of God; nay, ye received me with as much respect as if I had been Christ Jesus himself.

15 Great then was your happiness, and much did ye think yourselves obliged to me for the doctrines I taught you: For I bear you witness, that if it had been a thing allowable, and could have done me any good, ye would have plucked out your eyes, and have given them to me.

## Comment 4:12

### I beseech you

1. Up to this point he has been scathing: he has rebuked, called them fools, and crucifiers, but now he changes tactics.
2. The preacher is exhorted to use all methods.  I Tim. 4:2.

### Become as I am for I also became as ye are

1. Some think he means affection here.  "Feel toward me as I feel toward you."
a. MacKnight refers to II Chron. 18:3, where these expressions denote the most strict friendship.
b. It is certainly a personal appeal.
2. Others think 'I was a Jew zealously adicted to the law rites, etc., and became like you.'
3. Paul often apealed to brethren to imitate him.  I Cor. 4:16; 11:1; Phil. 3:17; II Thess. 3:7

### Ye did me no wrong (Ye have not injured me)

1. There is nothing personal in it.
2. The damage had been done to themselves.
3. They had withdrawn from Christ, it was more serious than some harm to Paul.

## Comment 4:13

### The first time

1. According to Acts 16:6; 18:23, Paul visited the region twice.
2. His illness had something to do with his preaching there on the first occasion.

### Because of an infirmity

1. Suggestions of what the infirmity was.
a. Perhaps it was a temporary illness.
b. Perhaps he never recovered from his blindness entirely.
c. Perhaps it was sorrow over death of his wife.
d. Perhaps a result of being beaten, etc.

2. Pauls infirmities mentioned.
a. II Cor. 12:9-10
b. II Cor. 11:23-25

## Comment 4:14

**And that which was a temptation to you in my flesh**
1. Perhaps they were tempted to kill him as they did in Lystra. Acts 14
2. Perhaps they tried to worship him as they did at Lystra. Acts 14:12
3. The Catholic Bible says, "a trial to you in the flesh."
a. He was a care to them — a burden.
b. As though he were a burden to them — housing, support, etc. This, to me . . . is strained.
4. The context in the following verses encourages one to believe that the events of Acts 14 might be referred to.
5. Whose temptation?
a. "My temptation" appears in several ancient manuscripts.
b. "Your temptation" appears in the Vulgate and Coptic.
c. Temptation — signifies trial of any kind.

**Ye despised not nor rejected —** (Literally: to spit out)
1. MacKnight "Yet my bodily infirmity which was a temptation to me, ye did not ridicule, neither did ye reject me with abhorrence as an imposter, but ye received me as an angel of God."
2. They did not despite the temptation to kill him at first, but sought to kill, or sought to worship him, is to be considered.
3. Perhaps it means "you did not despise my physical condition although you might have been tempted to do so."

**But ye received me as an angel of God.**
1. They demonstrated their zeal at Lystra.
a. Paul healed a cripple there. Acts 14:10
b. "When the multitude saw what Paul had done, they lifted up their voice, saying in the speech of Lycaonia, The gods are come down to us in the likeness of men." Acts 14:11
2. It is possible that this refers to their hospitality.

**Even as Christ Jesus**
1. Received him as of God, even as they did Jesus of God.
a. Worshipped him as they later did Christ — however this may not have been universal in Galatia.
b. They did receive him as universally as they did Christ and overlooked his infirmity.
2. Now they are not so enthusiastic.

## Comment 4:15

### Where then is that gratulation of yourselves?

(Where is then the blessedness ye spake of)
1. How much happier you used to be — for once you spoke of
your blessedness. (Clarke says no sentence is so variously
translated)
a. Having renounced the gospel you have lost your happiness.
b. Perhaps they had written to him telling in a joyful manner
their new position.
2. The word gratulation means, joy — congratulations.

### For I bear you witness

1. The good joy that you had was in relationship to me and the
gospel — not in the law.
2. Paul had seen joy with his own eyes, now they need not speak
of any other joy.

### That if possible ye would have plucked out your eyes and given them to me

1. Clarke says "Dearer than one's eyes" or "Give one's eyes"
was a proverbial saying.
2. Some think this was Paul's infirmity and they would have
given their eyes to him. McGarvey feels Paul speaks as though
he needed eyes.
3. Paul mentions a thorn in the flesh but does not name it.
II Cor. 12:7

## Study Questions 4:12-15

482. Does the word *beseech* indicate a change in Paul's method
to reach them?
483. Does he mean that they are now in a position that he left?
484. Was their falling a personal thing to Paul?
485. To whom was the damage of falling most harmful?
486. Did Christ suffer by their falling?
487. How was Paul infirmed?
488. Was it through infirmity, or because of it, that he preached?
489. Which preaching is referred to here?
490. Was he recuperating while there, and therefore preached
to them?
491. What temptation is referred to?
492. Did they originally have several attitudes toward Paul?

493. What events in Acts may be refered to?
494. Is Paul's temptation or their temptation refered to?
495. Do you suppose the Galatians knew exactly what was meant?
496. Explain "ye despised not nor rejected."
497. Tell of their acceptance of Paul as a heavenly being.
498. Could he be reminding them that they were a changeable people even in their attitude toward him?
499. Did they receive him as though he were Christ?
500. Define gratulation.
501. Has Paul accused them of losing their joy?
502. Explain "I bear you witness."
503. Were they once extremely devoted to Paul?
504. Does the mention of eyes indicate Paul had had eye trouble while in their presence?

## Text 4:16-20

**16 So then am I become your enemy, by telling you the truth?**

**17 They zealously seek you in no good way; nay, they desire to shut you out, that ye may seek them.  18 But it is good to be zealously sought in a good matter at all times, and not only when I am present with you.  19 My little children, of whom I am again in travail until Christ be formed in you—20 but I could wish to be present with you now, and to change my tone; for I am perplexed about you.**

## Paraphrase

16 So that, after all these expressions of affection and gratitude to me your spiritual father, ye think I am become your enemy now, when I inculcate the true doctrine of the gospel on you, and exhort you to adhere to it!

17 The teachers who have seduced you, pretend that they love you ardently; but they do not love you honourably; for they wish to exclude me, your spiritual father, from your affection, that ye may love them ardently, as the only faithful teachers of the gospel.

18 But ye should consider, that it is comely and commendable for you to be ardently in love with me, a good man, at all times, and not merely when I am present with you.

19 My beloved children in Christ, for whom I a second time travail in birth, till the knowledge, and temper, and virtues of Christ, be formed in you,

116

20 I could wish, indeed, to be present with you now, that I might suit my speech to your case; for I am altogether uncertain concerning you, how ye stand affected towards me; and feel the greatest anxiety on that account.

## Comment 4:16

**So then am I become your enemy, by telling you the truth?**
1. Truth should make people friends, not enemies.
a. Truth made you love me at the first.
b. Will truth now do otherwise?
2. False teachers always cause breaks in fellowship, yet denominationalism is honored in our religious society today.

## Comment 4:17

**They zealously seek you in no good way**
   (translated — they zealously affect you, but not well)
1. They had been "soft-soaped."
a. Satan's methods are clever: "by their smooth and fair speech they beguile the hearts of the innocent." Rom. 16:18
b. Zeal is not always backed with highest motives.
c. Some of the cruelest acts in history were done by sincere, zealous people, so zeal is not a criterion of truth.
2. It was a very selfish zeal.

**They desire to shut you out that ye may seek them**
1. They would exclude you, that ye might affect them.
2. "They count you — for no good motive, but they would estrange you, that you may court them." Dovay

**They**
1. Enemies of Paul and the Gospel are referred to.
2. False teachers were at work and Paul wanted them designated.

**Shut you out**
1. They would estrange you, or separate you from the gospel and from Paul.
2. When separated from Paul, the Galatians would then turn to the Judaiers for guidance.
3. At Antioch the Jews shut the Gentiles out of their fellowship. Gal. 2:13

## Comment 4:18

**it is good to be zealously sought in a good matter**
1. Paul of course in his absence is seeking them in a good matter.
2. The Catholic version differs here "Court the good from a good motive."

## Comment 4:19

**My little Children of whom I am again in travail**

1. Paul expressed himself kindly here. Cf. I Thess. 2:7,11
a. His children — refers to converts of his preaching.
b. "In Christ Jesus I begat you through the Gospel." I Cor. 4:15
2. Travail seems to mean great anxiety.

**Till Christ be formed**

1. They had lost Christ, their spiritual standing, freedom, and inheritance.
a. This sounds like "fallen from grace" not "once in grace always in grace."
b. Formed—wrought into the image of Christ.
2. Paul does not want to make merchandise of them; he is only concerned with their spiritual welfare.

## Comment 4:20

**But I could wish to be present with you now.**

1. This would help to counteract the presence of the false teachers.
a. He could travail in person.
b. He could speak in a new way. Cf. I Cor. 14:10 and Heb. 12:26
2. Would he speak in pleading tones, rebuking tones or would he speak with the tongue of an angel (I Cor. 13:1) to persuade them of the truth?

**And to change my tone**

1. Something is lacking in a written word.
a. He could change his voice according to their attitude.
b. He could speak more earnestly or tenderly, whatever the need might be.
2. He would change if it would help to challenge their thinking.

**For I am perplexed about you**

1. It is a marvel that they could be removed.
2. Paul's faith in human nature was disturbed.
3. Perplexed as a parent who knows not what to do with a wayward child.

## Study Questions 4:16-20

505. Do we make enemies by telling the truth?
506. What had truth done for them at first?
507. Is Paul reminding them that they ought not to be his enemies if he points out error in their life?

508. Can you be true and yet condemn error?
509. Had the false teaching been given casually?
510. Is zeal always the highest motive?
511. Can we trust zeal as a criterion of truth?
512. Explain "shut you out."
513. Of what would they be out?
514. Who is referred to by the word "they?"
515. Were they estranged from Paul? and therefore felt the need to turn to false teachers?
516. Is Paul zealously seeking them?
517. Does he mean that in his absence he is as zealous as when present?
518. Could he mean that they should zealously seek the truth of his letter?
519. How does Paul feel toward them in this verse?
520. In what way was he justified in calling them his children?
521. If Christ needed to be formed in them, were they in an extremely evil condition?
522. What did Paul mean by changing his tone, has he outdone it already?
523. Are there advantages in face to face discussions?
524. Is he confessing that their awful condition is one that requires great wisdom to handle?
525. Do we find human nature perplexing too?

3. Sarah and Hagar  4:21-31

### Text 4:21-24

**21 Tell me, ye that desire to be under the law, do ye not hear the law?  22 Fro it is written, that Abraham had two sons, one by the handmaid, and one by the free woman.  23 Howbeit the son by the handmaid is born after the flesh; but the son by the free woman is born through promise.  24 Which things contain an allegory: for these women are two covenants; one from mount Sinai, bearing children unto bondage, which is Hagar.**

### Paraphrase

21 Tell me, ye who wish to be under the law of Moses as the rule of your justification, why do ye not understand the law, which teaches that Abraham's children by faith, who are heirs of the promises, are free from the bondage of the law?

22 For it is written in the law, that Abraham, the father of the people of God, had two sons; one by the bond-maid Hagar, and one by the free-woman Sarah, his wife.

23 But he, verily, who was of the bond-maid, was begotten by the natural strength of his parents, and being born a slave, had no title to inherit his father's estate: But he who was of the free-woman, was begotten through the strength supernaturally communicated to his parents by the promise, "Lo, Sarah thy wife shall have a son," and like his mother being free, was his father's heir.

24 Which things, concerning the sons and wives of Abraham, and the power by which these sons were begotten, and the state into which they were born, are an allegory. For these women, as the mothers of Abraham's children, are types of the two Covenants, by which men become the church and people of God. The one is that verily, which was given from Mount Sinai, which made Abraham's posterity by Isaac only the visible church and people of God, and bringeth forth its children into bondage to the law; which covenant it fitly represented by Hagar, who brought forth her son Ishmael into bondage.

### Comment 4:21

**Tell me**

1. Here Paul invites them to think seriously about an allegory.
2. After the lesson is presented they are to answer his question.

**Ye that desire to be under the law**

1. Have you really read and heard the law?
2. Those who understand the Scripture can see a deeper meaning behind the Scripture.
a. Therefore Paul is challenging their very best.
b. They needed to heed II Tim. 2:15.

**Hear the law**

1. It is as though Paul would end his agrument in verse 20, but he decides to give them a lesson from the law itself.
2. The law has a wide meaning as seen by Paul's use of the term.
a. Mosaic institutions — those that they were returning to.
b. Pentateuch — where the history is recorded to which the apostle refers.
3. Scripture is clear —therefore heed it — don't treat it like the false teachers do.

## Comment 4:22

### For it is written

1. The Scriptures bear witness.
a. See Gen. 16:15
b. See Gen. 21:2
2. This was the method of Jesus — appealing to God.

### That Abraham had two sons

1. The Sons were symbolic.
a. Ishmael was born of a bond-maid — Hagar.
b. Isaac was born of a free woman — Sarah.
2. Paul emphasizes that Sarah is "the free woman."
a. She is mentioned four times as a free woman without calling her by name.
b. Sarah was a princess in name and held a prominent place in history as the mother of Israel.
c. She is the type of the New covenant and the covenant of freedom.
3. Hagar is the symbol of the bond woman.
a. Physical descent from Abraham is not what is decisive, but spiritual affinity to him.
b. The children who go back to the law, go back to the woman and her son born in bondage.

## Comment 4:23

### Howbeit the son by the handmaid

1. This is Ishmael — who was not of promise.
2. He was born a slave and came into the world according to the usual course of nature.
3. Ishmael persecuted Isaac and so in Paul's day, the progency of the law persecuted the children of the gospel.

### Born through promise

1. Isaac was born after the age of procreation had passed.
2. His birth was supernatural.

## Comment 4:24

### An Allegory

1. From two words meaning "another" and "to Speak."
2. This, signifies a thing that is representative of another.
3. Here, it is a representative of a spiritual meaning.

**For these women are two covenants**

1. Hagar typifies Sinai, the old covenant — bondage.
2. Sarah typifies the Messiah, the new covenant — freedom.

## Study Questions 4:21-24

526. Is Paul enforcing the law on them, since they seem to prefer it?
527. How is the word law used by the apostle? Does it always refer to Moses, to the 10 Commandments?
528. Where is the scripture found that Paul quotes?
529. Who were Abraham's sons?
530. How are the mothers described?
531. Who was born after the flesh?
532. Was his birth natural or supernatural?
533. Why did God allow this and fail to condemn it, or did He?
534. What was miraculous about the birth of Isaac?
535. How is his birth a part of the promise?
536. Define allegory.
537. What is represented?
538. Is a physical seed automatically a child of the promise?
539. Define covenants.

## Text 4:25-27

**25 Now this Hagar is mount Sinai in Arabia, and answereth to the Jerusalem that now is: for she is in bondage with her children. 26 But the Jerusalem that is above is free, which is our mother. 27 For it is written, Rejoice, thou barren that bearest not; Break forth and cry, thou that travailest not: For more are the children of the desolate than of her that hath the husband.**

## Paraphrase

25 Hagar, the bond-maid, is a fit type of the covenant from Sinai, (for Hagar is one of the names of Mount Sinai in Arabia, from whence that covenant was given); and she, with her son, representeth the present Jerusalem or Jewish church, which was formed on that covenant, and is in bondage to the law, with the Jews her children.

26 But the catholic church, consisting of believers of all nations, which is formed on the covenant published from Mount Zion, and which I call the Jerusalem above, because its most perfect state will be in heaven, is represented by the free-woman Sarah, who is the mother of us all who believe.

27 My interpretation of the things respecting Abraham's wives and sons is not new; it is alluded to by Isaiah: For (Chp. Liv. 1) it is written, "Sing, O barren, thou that didst not bear, break forth into singing and cry aloud, thou that didst not travail with child: for more are the children of the desolate, than the children of the married wife, saith the Lord."

## Comment 4:25

### Now this Hagar is Mt. Sinai

(some manuscripts read "For Sinai is a Mountain in Arabia.")

1. This is a passage with many varied readings in the manuscripts and this is discussed at some length by MacKnight in his epistle on p. 300.
2. A question is, "Is he talking about a woman or a mountain?"
a. The problem centers in the fact that there is such a mountain.
b. Mathew Henry says, "Sinai was called Agar or Hagar by the Arabians."
c. MacKnight quotes Gratius as saying that there was a city in the mountain range named Hagar. (p. 83)
1) Its inhabitants were called Hagarenes.
2) The word *Hagar* signifies rock, and Sinai is sometimes called *Rock*. See Exodus 33:22
d. A study of context clarifies that point.
3. A question could be, "Is he talking about the Hagarenes or is he discussing Abraham's handmaid?"
a. He surely is talking about Hagar.
b. Hagar the bondmaid is a fit type of the covenant from Sinai, for Hagar is one of the names of Mt. Sinai, in Arabia, from whence that covenant was given, and she, with her son, represented the present Jerusalem or Jewish church which was formed on that covenant, and is in bondage to the law, with the Jews as her children.

## Comment 4:26

### The Jerusalem that is above

1. This Jerusalem is the church.
2. These are the children of promise.
3. Sarah is the mother of all believers, on account of her bringing forth Isaac supernaturally by virtue of the promise.

**Is free**

1. The law can be generally spoken of as bondage.
a. Peter said, "Now therefore why make ye trial of God, that ye should put a yoke upon the neck of the disciples which neither our fathers nor we were able to bear?" Acts 15:10
b. Jesus accused those under the law of making more serious demands. "Yea, they bind heavy burdens and grievous to be borne, and lay them on men's shoulders; but they themselves will not move them with their finger." Matt. 23:4
2. Freedom is a characteristic of those in Christ.

**Our Mother**

1. Hagar is one mother — Sarah is the other, and she brings forth children unto freedom.
2. Sarah answers to the Jerusalem above.
3. This Jerusalem above is a free woman, who is the mother of us all.

## Comment 4:27

**For it is written**

1. This proceeds to quote Isaiah 54:1
2. Paul is saying "My interpretation of the things respecting Abraham's wives and sons is not in error for it is alluded to by Isaiah."

**Rejoice, thou barren that bearest not**

1. Sarah was the barren one, but she had occasion to rejoice.
2. Isaiah may have alluded to Gen. 17:15-16 where God said concerning her, "She shall be a mother of nations" and by changing her name from Sarai into Sarah, confirmed the promise as he did to Abraham.
a. Abram — "exalted father" was changed to Abraham — "Father of a multitude."
b. Sarai — "My princess" was changed to Sarah "Princess."
3. The gospel covenant with Abraham was a long time barren like Sarah.

**Break forth and cry, thou that travailest not**

1. The cry here must refer to a cry of joy, rather than sorrow.
2. Sarah had no travail in childbirth, but the promise was given and finally was carried out.
3. The promise to Abraham was not born for centuries — but Isaiah is stating the coming birth of Gentiles.

**For more are the children of the desolate**

1. Hagar no doubt calls Sarah the destered wife, because when Abraham found her barren he deserted her, with her consent, to bring forth a child with Hagar.
2. A large family is prophecied by Isaiah 800 years before Christ.

**Than of her that hath the husband**

1. Hagar seemed to have the husband, since Sarah was barren.
2. Isaiah prophecied that the Christians would outnumber those born under the law as typified by Hagar.

## Study Questions 4:25-27

540. What does he say Sinai is?
541. How is Sinai located in Arabia, yet likened into Jerusalem in Syria?
542. Is he talking about a woman, a mountain, or both?
543. Could Agar and Hagar be the same?
544. What is the point that we must not miss in this discussion?
545. Has he used two Jerusalems to make his point?
546. Is Jerusalem our mother, or Sarah?
547. What woman was free?
548. Do we speak of cities as feminine?
549. What mother should the Galatians claim?
550. Does Paul have any scripture for his allegory?
551. What did Isaiah say?
552. Was Sarah's name changed?
553. Is the cry one of desolation or joy?
554. Was Sarah the wife described as desolate?
555. Which wife would have the most children or descendants?
556. Is this the reason for the cry of the one not in travail?

## Text 4:28-31

**28 Now we, brethren, as Isaac was, are children of promise. 29 But as then he that was born after the flesh persecuted him that was born after the Spirit, so also it is now. 30 Howbeit what saith the scripture? Cast out the handmaid and her son: for the son of the handmaid shall not inherit with the son of the freewoman. 31 Wherefore, brethren, we are not children of a handmaid, but of the freewoman.**

125

## Paraphrase

28 We therefore, brethren, who believe, even though we are not related to Abraham by natural descent, after the manner of Isaac, are children to Abraham and to Sarah by the promise, which made him the father, and her the mother of nations.

29 But even as it happened then, that Ishmael, who was begotten according to the flesh — begotten by the natural strength of his parents, and related to Abraham by natural descent only —persecuted Isaac, who was begotten according to the Spirit, and resembled his father Abraham in the dispositions of his mind, so also it hath happened now, the Jews the natural seed persecute us the spiritual seed.

30 But what saith the scripture? "She said unto Abraham, cast out this bond-woman and her son; for the son of this bond-woman shall not be heir with my son, even with Isaac. And God said to Abraham, in all that Sarah hath said unto thee, hearken to her voice: For in Isaac shall thy seed be called."

31 Well then, brethren, it appears from the law itself, that we who by faith are Abraham's sons, are not children of the bond-maid Hagar, but of the free-woman Sarah; and as her children, we are heirs of the promises, although not in bondage to the law.

## Comment 4:28

### Children of promise

1. Paul is drawing a conclusion that the Gentiles would understand if they were Christian.
2. The Christian is in the promise to Abraham just as Isaac was.
3. They are children, not in a genealogical sense but in a spiritual sense.
4. Three qualities of Isaac:   1. A promised child. Gen. 17:16
                                     2. An obedient child. Gen. 22:9
                                     3. A fruitful child and man. Gen. 25:11

## Comment 4:29

### he that . . . . persecuted him

1. Ishmael persecuted Isaac.
2. This persecution refers to Gen. 21:8-9 when Abraham made a great feast the day Isaac was weaned.
3. On this occasion Sarah caught Ishmael mocking.

**him that was born after the Spirit**
1. This refers to the supernatural birth of Isaac.
2. It reminds us of the statement made to Joseph concerning his wife to be — Mary. "For that which is conceived in her is of the Holy Spirit." Matt. 1:20

**So it is now**
1. Judaizers were causing trouble in Galatia. See 2:13
2. The Jews made trouble constantly for the Apostles and evangelists.
3. Jews followed Paul and stirred up trouble.
a. The Jews stirred up trouble for him in Thessolonica. Acts 17:5-9
b. The Jews followed him to Berea and stirred up trouble there. Acts 17:11
c. The Jews mobbed him in the city of Jerusalem. Acts 21:27-33

## Special Study

### Galatians 4:21-31    Sarah and Hagar Compared

I. Mothers
   1. Handmaid..........Old Covenant — vs. 24
   2. Freewoman........New Covenant — vs. 26-31

II. Sons
   1. Personalities
   a. Ishmael........Jewish persecution of Christian — vs. 29
   b. Isaac...........Christian non-retaliation
   2. Births
   a. Ishmael........Natural birth — vs. 29
   b. Isaac ...........Spiritual birth — Gen. 18:10; Gal. 14:29

III. Dispensation
   1. Ishmael........Characteristic of Jews under law in Old Covenant
   2. Isaac ...........Characteristic of New Covenant

IV. State
   1. Ishmael........State of bondage — vs. 25
   2. Isaac ...........State of freedom — vs. 31

V. Results
   1. Ishmael........Rejection of Jews — vs. 30
   2. Isaac ...........Acceptance of Christian — vs. 30

## Comment 4:30

### Howbeit what saith the scripture

1. This is a good question to ask in any religious problems.
2. Many preachers run to their creeds and books of discipline instead of to the Scripture.
3. Paul quotes from Gen. 21:10-12.

### Cast out the handmaid and her son

1. Sarah demanded this as punishment for Ishmael's mocking of Isaac. Gen. 21:8-9
2. Paul is stating that the present Jerusalem and her children shall be cast out and shall not be heirs with the sons of the free woman.
3. The Jews were rejected because they did not come to God by faith.
4. This was literally fulfilled in a very physical sense too.
a. The Jews caused constant trouble for Christians, but it came to an end.
b. Jerusalem was destroyed by Titus in 70 A.D. and like Hagar and Ishmael the Jews were cast out.

### For the son of the handmaid shall not inherit with the son

1. The enemies could fight against scripture but they, like Ishmael, will be driven out of the fellowship of God.
2. A loss of inheritance should be a challenging word, to answer the Galatians.

### The son of the freewoman

1. The Jew can not inherit with the Christian until he comes by faith into the promise.
2. We must not go back to the law for it is bondage and loss.

## Comment 4:31

### We are not children of the handmaid

1. This is plain language.
2. Why now are the Galatians going back to the children who are cast out and who are bound to lose the inheritance?

### But of the freewoman

1. This is a privilege of birth which we may choose.
2. The promise of freedom and inheritance should be attractive to all who heed "what is written."

## Study Questions 4:28-31

557. Who is the Christian likened unto?
558. In what way are we children of promise?
559. Could Gentiles without an Old Testament understand this argument quickly?
560. Do you suppose that these people had a good knowledge of Abraham before Paul discussed this subject with them? Why?
561. Can a person be a sincere Jew and have the blessing of Christ?
562. Who is the "he" of the verse?
563. Who is the "him" of Paul's discussion?
564. Do we have a record of this persecution?
565. Who caught Ishmael mocking?
566. Who had the spiritual birth?
567. Did Paul observe a similarity in persecution, and what was it?
568. Were the Jews busy at making trouble for the apostle everywhere?
569. Is Paul's frequent use of scripture a good example for all religious discussions?
570. What did Paul quote in this case?
571. Who did the casting in this case?
572. Was Paul suggesting that some casting out should take place in Galatia?
573. Were the Jews eventually cast down by God in Jerusalem?
574. Is the child of the handmaid cast out forever?
575. Who is the "we" referred to here?
576. Is salvation free to the sons of the freewoman?
577. Has God made salvation possible for the children of the woman who was cast out?
578. Do we have the privilege to choose what woman will be our mother spiritually?

## Questions on Galatians, Chapter Four

### True - False

_____ 1. Paul states that the heir, when a child, is no different than a servant until the time the father appoints. Vs. 1
_____ 2. The apostle condemns the Galatians for observing days, months, seasons and years.

_____ 3. The children of Abraham were not all of the same covenant in Paul's allegory.

_____ 4. The Christian is the child of the free woman in Paul's figure.

_____ 5. Paul asked the Galatians that he not be considered an enemy for telling them the truth.

_____ 6. The reason we are free from the law is because Christ was not born under the law.

_____ 7. The reason the church in America is strong is because its members are descendants from the Galatians who were so faithful.

_____ 8. Paul reminds the Galatians that he was once dearer to them than their own eyes.

_____ 9. Since Christ was not under the law, he did not redeem those under it, but left that responsibility to God.

_____10. Paul was confident that his labors among the Galatians had not been in vain.

_____11. Paul stated the Galatians had done him a personal evil in their religious difficulties. (vs. 12)

_____12. Paul felt that he need not be present with them since the Galatian letter would be delivered shortly.

_____13. Paul speaks of the two sons of Abraham and says these things contain an allegory.

_____14. A rightful heir assumes all rights and privileges at birth.

_____15. Paul said "become as I am, for I also am become as you are."

_____16. Abraham's two wives were Sarah and Hagar.

_____17. God acts without taking time into consideration.

_____18. Paul evidently was a very rugged person as seen by his many travels, and no mention of any infirmity.

_____19. Those who were courting the Galatians were not doing it for a wholesome purpose.

_____20. The Galatians were reminded that they once were treated as an angel. (vs. 14)

_____21. Paul said that he could wish to be present with them and to change his tone.

_____22. Because we are sons God sent forth the Spirit of His Son into our hearts. (vs. 6)

_____23. A strange figure of Paul is spoken when he says the Jerusalem that is above is free and is our mother. (v. 26)
_____24. We Christians are as Isaac was, Children of promise.
_____25. The one born after the flesh persecuted him that was born after the Spirit and Paul says so it is now. (v. 29)

### PART THREE

# APPEAL TO STEADFASTNESS, FAITHFULNESS AND DUTY
## 5:1 - 6:18

A. LIBERTY OF THE GOSPEL 5:1-12

1. Freedom and Responsibility 5:1

### Text 5:1

**1 For freedom did Christ set us free: stand fast therefore, and be not entangled again in a yoke of bondage.**

### Paraphrase

1 Because believers are the children of the free-woman, do ye Gentiles stand fast in the freedom from the law of Moses, wherewith Christ hath freed us in the gospel dispensation, and be not a second time held fast in the yoke of bondage, as if it were necessary to salvation.

### Comment 5:1

**For freedom did Christ set us free**

1. How do we obtain freedom?
a. "Ye shall know the truth, and the truth shall make you free." John 8:32
b. "If therefore the Son shall make you free, ye shall be free indeed." John 8:36
2. In what ways are we free?
a. Free from sin. ". . . and being made free from sin." Rom. 6:18
b. Free from death. "made me free from the law of sin and of death." Rom. 8:2
c. Free from religious oppression.
1) Paul emphasized that in this book.
a. "to spy out our liberty." Gal. 2:4
b. "I through the law died unto the law." Gal. 2:19
2) Jesus condemned religious oppression.
a. "Yea, they bind heavy burdens and grievous to be borne . . . make broad their phylacteries (charms) and enlarge the borders of their garments." Matt. 23:4,5
3. Christ bought our freedom with a great price. I Cor. 7:22,23

131

### stand fast therefore

1. When we attain a position of freedom, it should be maintained.
a. The Galatians were being moved by a crafty Jewish force.
b. We have denominational forces seeking to move us out of freedom in the New Testament Church.
2. *Stand fast* is a common exhortation in the N. T.
a. "Watch ye, stand fast in the faith." I Cor. 16:13
b. "Stand fast in one spirit." Phil. 1:27
c. "Stand fast in the Lord." Phil. 4:1
d. "If ye stand fast in the Lord." I Thess. 3:8
e. "Stand fast and hold the traditions." II Thess. 2:15

### and be not entangled

1. Affairs of this life entangle one.
a. "No soldier on service entangleth himself in the affairs of this life." II Tim. 2:4
b. The world would have us so busy, that no time would be left to do the Lord's will.
c. Preachers sometimes are so used by the Red Cross, Y.M.C.A. organizations, etc., that they have no time for soul winning.
2. The entanglements of the past life are frightful.
a. "If they are again entangled . . . the last state is become worse than the first." II Peter 2:20

### in a yoke

1. The yoke referred to here is the law that Jews were putting on the neck of free Gentile Christians.
"Put a yoke upon the neck of the disciples." Acts 15:10
2. Sin is a yoke: "Everyone that committeth sin is the bond-servant of sin." John 8:34
3. The only yoke for us is that of Jesus. "Take my yoke upon you." Matt. 11:29-30

### of bondage

1. This is slavery—this is a condition in which there is no sonship and inheritance.
2. Christ liberated slaves but foolish people went back to bondage.
3. The Christian has freedom to be a slave in a new sense.
a. "Servants of righteousness." Romans 6:18
b. "Servants unto God." Romans 6:22
c. "Serveth Christ." Romans 14:18

d. "Serve the Lord Christ." Col. 3:24
e. Service from the heart. Eph. 6:6

## Study Questions 5:1

579. What is implied in verse 1 — "entangled again in a yoke of bondage?"
580. How do we obtain freedom?
581. In what ways are we free?
582. Are we free from religious oppression?
583. What do you understand by "stand fast therefore?"
584. Is it a common exhortation?
585. Were they to stand firm in freedom?
586. How does Christ set us free?
587. Were the Galatians entangled before they were Christians?
588. In what danger of entanglement were they?
589. Can a person be entangled in a good thing too, but to his detriment?
590. What is a yoke?
591. Describe the yoke involved here.
592. Were Jews able to yoke Gentile Christians?
593. Should the Christian wear a good yoke, and if so what?

2. Alternatives of Entanglement and Freedom 5:2-6

## Text 5:2-6

**2 Behold, I Paul say unto you, that, if ye receive circumcision, Christ will profit you nothing. 3 Yea, I testify again to every man that receiveth circumcision, that he is a debtor to do the whole law. 4 Ye are severed from Christ, ye who would be justified by the law; ye are fallen away from grace. 5 For we through the Spirit by faith wait for the hope of righteousness. 6 For in Christ Jesus neither circumcision availeth anything, nor uncircumcision; but faith working through love.**

## Paraphrase

2 Behold, I Paul say to you, that if ye be circumcised as a condition necessary to your salvation, the death of Christ will profit you nothing.

3 And, though ye have been taught otherwise by the Judaizers, I testify, moreover, to every circumcised person who seeks justification by the law, that he is bound to perform the whole law of Moses perfectly; and if he fails, he subjects himself to the curse. (Gal. 3:10)

133

4 Ye have renounced Christ as a Saviour, who seek to be justified by the law of Moses; consequently ye shall receive no benefit from his death: Ye have excluded yourselves from the free gift of justification offered to you in the gospel.

5 But we believers, the spiritual seed of Abraham, whom God hath promised to justify through the gifts of the Spirit, which are the evidence of our adoption, look for the hoped righteousness by faith to be bestowed on us as a free gift at the general judgment.

6 For in the gospel dispensation, neither circumcision availeth any thing towards our acceptance with God, nor uncircumcision, but faith strongly working by love to God and to man.

## Comment 5:2

**Behold, I Paul**
1. I, Who have received the Gospel not from men.
2. I, called to preach the gospel with authority.
3. He is not stating this as a personal opinion but to give his statement credence.

**if ye receive circumcision, Christ will profit you nothing**
1. Christ becomes worthless: if He is not everything, then He is nothing.
2. Circumcision in itself is nothing.
3. Yet the Galatians looked to it and the covenant it represented for justification—they forfeited everything in Christ.
a. It is not so much one thing—but a principle.
b. If they seek justification by the works of the law, then they renounce justification through faith.

## Comment 5:3

**every man that receiveth circumcision, that he is a debtor to do the whole law.**
1. If you submit to one, then you are obligated to all the law, for one commandment or phrase is no more binding than another.
2. Thus we have two things wrong.
a. It makes Christ uprofitable.
b. It obligates one to do all the law.
3. Circumcision was a seal of covenant relationship, and the covenant obligates one to do it all.
4. Why did Paul have Timothy to submit? See Acts 15:3

a. It was not for Timothy's salvation.
b. It was an expediency in preaching.
5. The law is indivisible — it is not to be observed partially.

## Comment 5:4

### ye are severed from Christ

Catholic Bible — *ye are estranged from Christ*
King James — *Christ is become of no effect unto you*
1. In seeking justification by works of the law, you go into apostasy.
a. This sounds like once saved, not always saved.
b. You must have the law and no Christ—or Christ and no law.
c. A person can be cut off, if Jesus meant what He said. "If a man abide not in me, he is cast forth as a branch, and is withered; and they gather them, and cast them into the fire, and they are burned." John 15:6

### who would be justified by the law

1. This was the choice of some.
2. They had the privilege to choose the law.

### Ye are fallen from grace

1. Yet some say, there is no falling after salvation has been received.
2. When you fall in the ocean, it matters not which side of the ship you fall from — you are in the ocean and lost.
3. To fall from grace means to lose the atonement, the forgiveness of sins, righteousness, liberty and the life.
4. To lose the grace means to gain the wrath, and judgment of God, death, the bondage of the devil and condemnation.

## Comment 5:5

### we through the Spirit by faith wait

1. How do we wait?
a. Through His instruction of divine revelation.
1) John 14:1-6
2) "Every scripture inspired of God." II Tim. 3:16
3) "them that preached the gospel unto you by the Holy Spirit sent forth from heaven." I Peter 1:12
4) "For no prophecy ever came by the will of man: but men spake from God, being moved by the Holy Spirit." II Peter 1:21

5) "The spirit himself beareth witness." Rom. 8:16

a. We have to know God's words else we would not know to wait for God's blessings.

b. Hope makes our waiting worthwhile.

b. Through His indwelling presence we wait patiently.

2. How else could you wait? The faithless do not wait.

a. The Galatians were trusting in carnal ordinances.

b. Their faith was not on the proper source for inheritance.

### for the hope of righteousness

1. What is the difference in faith and hope? (See Luther pg. 203)

a. They differ in their origin.

1) Faith originates in the understanding.

2) Hope arises in the will.

b. They differ in function.

1) Faith teaches, describes, directs.

2) Hope exhorts the mind to be strong, courageous.

c. They differ in their objectives.

1) Faith concentrates on the truth.

2) Hope looks to the goodness of God.

d. They differ in sequence.

1) Faith is the beginning of life before tribulation. Hebrews 11

2) Hope comes later and is born of tribulation. Rom. 5

e. They differ in regard to their effect.

1) Faith is a judge; it judges error.

2) Hope is a soldier; it fights against tribulations, the cross, despondency, despair, and waits for better things.

a. By faith we begin; by hope we endure.

b. Hope without faith is blind arrogance because it lacks knowledge.

2. Faith, hope and love are the three greatest of Christian virtues, I Cor. 13:13.

### hope of righteousness

1. This may have the same meaning as Peter's statement, "receiving the end of your faith, even the salvation of your souls." I Peter 1:9

2. In this realm there will be no sin, but righteousness. Rev. 21:27; 22:15

## Comment 5:6

### neither circumcision availeth anything, nor uncircumcision

1. A person's physical condition in relationship to Abraham matters not.
2. The valuable thing is faith in Christ and circumcision is of no value.

### Faith working through love

1. The valuable faith is one that works through love.
a. Faith without works is dead. See James 2:17
1) Idle faith is not justifying faith.
b. Faith without love is nothing. "If I have all faith, so as to remove mountains, but have not love, I am nothing." I Cor. 13:2
2. If loving service is not manifested, the Christian is no better than a Galatian depending upon circumcision.

## Study Questions 5:2-6

594. When Paul mentions self as in verse two, does he lessen the authority of his word?
595. If Christ is not worth everything, is He worth anything?
596. Why was circumcision an issue?
597. If Christ is our Saviour, do we need to depend upon observances, rituals, etc., to save us?
598. Why does obedience to one law demand obedience to all?
599. If circumcision is a seal, then would it demand that a person go all the way?
600. Why did Paul have Timothy circumcised?
601. Do we have a right to expediencies in order to win some to Christ?
602. What does the word *severed* mean?
603. Is it the same as apostasy?
604. Can we say that it is falling from grace?
605. Does this verse destroy the "once in grace, always in grace" theory?
606. What other ways is the word *severed* translated?
607. Did Jesus say that a person can be cut off? Cf. John 15:1-6.
608. What would do the severing?
609. Were they responsible for their own severing?
610. Does Paul say that a man can fall from grace?

611. What all is involved when a person falls?
612. Does he lose the atonement, the forgiveness, eternal life?
613. Will a person have punishment for severing himself?
614. How much false teaching may one accept to sever him from Christ?
615. How do we wait?
616. What is the Christian waiting for?
617. Is the waiting a time of indolence?
618. Two words are used that are similar. What is the difference between faith and hope?
619. What has the Spirit to do with our waiting?
620. Describe the hope of righteousness.
621. Is hope of righteousness different from hope of the righteous?
622. Will there be righteousness where the Christian is going?
623. Does Christ make void both circumcision and uncircumcision?
624. What is the one availing thing?
625. What does Paul connect with faith here?
626. Does the faith he describes do work?
627. What is the motive of the work?
628. If we work with any other motive, is it worthwhile? Cf. I Cor. 13.

3. A Word of Protest 5:7-12

## Text 5:7-9

**7 Ye were running well; who hindered you that ye should not obey the truth? 8 This persuasion came not of him that calleth you. 9 A little leaven leaveneth the whole lump.**

## Paraphrase

7 At first ye made great progress in the doctrine and practice of the gospel: Who hath interrupted you in that good course, so as to make you now reject the truth?

8 This persuasion concerning the law, and the efficacy of its expiation, is not wrought in you by him who first called you.

9 A little leaven, that is, the errors of one teacher, are sufficient to corrupt a whole church.

## Comment 5:7

**ye were running well**

1. The Christian life is like a race. "Know ye not that they that run in a race run all, but one receiveth the prize? Even so run; that ye may attain." I Cor. 9:24

"Therefore let us also, seeing we are compassed about with so great a cloud of witnesses, lay aside every weight and the sin which doth so easily beset us; and let us run with patience the race that is set before us . . ." Heb. 12:1

2. Faith is to advance one, not to retreat him to bondage.

### who hindered you

1. A good question to ask backsliders. Heb. 6:4-6
2. It should apply to many situations.
a. Friends in bad company: "Evil companionships." I Cor. 15:33
b. Loved ones: "Loveth father or mother more." Matt. 10:37
c. Job: "Five yoke of oxen." Luke 14:19
d. Possessions: "It is easier for a camel to go through a needle's eye." Mark 10:24-25
e. False teachers: "or an angel from heaven." Gal. 1:8-9
3. McGarvey says *hindered* is a military term — an army embarrassed by destroyed bridges and roads.
4. Here are examples of those who ran but failed.
a. Lot's wife. Gen. 19:26
b. Rich young ruler. Matt. 19:20
c. Annanias and Sapphira. Acts 5:1-11

### that ye should not obey the truth

1. Obedience to the steps of salvation is not sufficient; you are disobedient if you backslide, just as though you had never done them.
2. To accept false teaching is the same as disobedience.

## Comment 5:8

### This persuasion came not of him that calleth you

1. The persuasion of obedience to Moses is referred to.
2. The devil is a cunning persuader.
a. He beguiled Eve with desire to know, as God knows good and evil. Gen. 3:6
1) She was tricked by food that was good to eat.
2) She was tricked by a delight to the eyes.
3) She was lured by the desire to be wise.
b. The devil persuaded Judas to betray Christ.
3. "Him that called you" — must refer to Christ.
a. Paul has made it plain that they have departed from Christ and no doubt He is the one Paul means here.

b. It would not be needful to say, "the persuasion came not from Paul," but MacKnight holds that Paul is meant.

### Comment 5:9

**A little leaven leaveneth the whole lump**

1. Leaven is used of both good and evil in scripture.
a. Evil. Matt. 16:6; I Cor. 5:7-8
b. Good. Matt. 13:33

2. Paul is trying to make them see the danger of a small deviation.
a. They might have first said "What if we deviate a little from Paul?"
b. To tolerate a trifling error inevitably leads to heresy.
c. We have no right to trifle with the Bible.
d. Small faults grow to be big ones.

3. Hear James on the matter: "For whosoever shall keep the whole law, and yet stumble in one point, he is become guilty of all." James 2:10

### Study Questions 5:7-9

629. Does Paul mean that the Christian life is like a race?
630. Is disobedience a failure to run?
631. How long had they been running well?
632. Does Paul know who hindered them?
633. What kind of thing does the devil use on us to hinder us?
634. What kind of term is the word hindered?
635. Give example of those who ran for God, but were hindered.
636. Is backsliding the same as disobedience in this verse?
637. Is acceptance of false teaching equivalent to falling from the truth and disobedience?
638. Who persuaded whom?
639. Is it a persuasion to Moses or Christ?
640. Is the devil a shrewd persuader?
641. Is the one who called — Christ or Paul?
642. Is leaven used to symbolize both good and evil?
643. Is leaven in this case evil?
644. Does Paul establish that a small heresy may be very serious?
645. Should we consider a small deviation to be very dangerous?
646. If small faults grow to be great ones, is it profitable for small untruths to do the same?

## Text 5:10-12

**10** I have confidence to you-ward in the Lord, that ye will be none otherwise minded: but he that troubleth you shall bear his judgment, whosoever he be. **11** But I, brethren, if I still preach circumcision, why am I still persecuted? then hath the stumbling-block of the cross been done away? **12** I would that they that unsettle you would even go beyond circumcision.

## Paraphrase

10 However, to comfort you, I am persuaded concerning you by the Lord, that on reading what I have written, ye will not think differently from me concerning the doctrine of justification by faith: But the teacher who, by his falsehoods, hath given you so much trouble, shall, when I come, be punished for it, whosoever he be.

11 My enemies tell you, that I preach circumcision. But I, brethren, if I now preach circumcision, why am I now persecuted by the Jews? Having left off preaching salvation through a crucified Messiah, certainly the offence of the cross is removed, (I Cor. 1:23), and they should no longer persecute me.

12 I wish they were even cut off by excommunication, who subvert your faith by their malicious calumnies and false doctrines.

## Comment 5:10

**I have confidence to you-ward in the Lord**

1. This is a sincere hope that they take the safe view of the subject and avoid the trouble caused by false teachers.
2. If they accept the Lord's sacrifice as sufficient for their salvation, Paul's confidence is well grounded.

**none otherwise minded**

1. That you will have the mind of Christ (in the Lord).
a. Paul expresses confidence that they will take the same view of the situation that he does. See Phil. 2:5
b. In this way they may avoid the contamination of the leaven.
2. Always the mind of Christ is needed in every problem.
3. If Church problems are not settled in the Lord, the Church stands as a reproach to the Lord in the commandments.

**but he that troubleth you shall bear his judgment**

1. For having sown tares in the wheat, some person will pay in the judgment.

2. We are to have a specific attitude toward false teachers.
a. "Let him be anathema." Gal. 1:8-9
b. "Receive him not into your house." II John 9,10
3. God will punish them, it is not our business. See II Cor. 10:6-8; 13:10

## Comment 5:11

**if I still preach circumcision**

1. Evidently Paul had been accused of preaching it.
2. Perhaps it was because of his having Timothy circumcised. Acts 16:3

**why am I still persecuted**

1. It was his antagonism to circumcision that brought persecution.
2. False teachers preached circumcision and thus retained the favor of the Jews.
3. David found that truth cost. "I believe for I will speak: I was greatly afflicted." Ps. 116:10
4. Jesus prophecied persecution. Matt. 10:16-23
5. Jesus told us how to face it. Matt. 5:12

**then hath the stumbling block of the Cross been done away,**

1. Is this a question or an affirmation?
a. It probably is affirmation. The cross was a stumbling block to the Jews because it removed the obligation of the law.
b. At this point I can not be most certain — except that the cross is a stumbling block. Cf. I Cor. 1:23
2. If Paul had preached the cross along with circumcision, it would not be such a stumbling block.
3. There would be no need for trouble if he preached both. It is the cancellation of the law by the cross that causes trouble.

## Comment 5:12

**I would that they that unsettle you**

(I would they were even cut off which troubleth you, King James.)
1. Paul had strong feelings against those who would run out on the course and disturb the Christian runners.
a. Hindering and unsettling are of the same idea.
b. Causing a stumbling is serious according to Christ. See Matt. 18:6
2. The next phrase tells what Paul wishes in regard to the false teacher.

**would even go beyond circumcision**

1. Some think that Paul is referring to castration here.
a. Some Greek cults practiced this.
b. The priest of Attica and Cybele were castrated.
c. Castration was prohibited by the Law. Cf. Deut. 23:1
2. Paul equated circumcision and the pagan practices as both foreign to Christ.
a. The purpose of both was to receive righteousness.
b. A heathen and a judaiser therefore stood condemned, for the motive was evil.

## Galatians — Expository Outlines
### Five views at the Cross

1. Crucified with Christ — "I have been crucified with Christ; and it is no longer I that live." Gal. 2:20
2. Christ crucified for me — Gal. 3:1
3. Flesh crucified in me — "They that are of Christ Jesus have crucified the flesh with the passions and the lusts thereof." Gal. 5:24
4. World Crucified unto me — "Far be it from me to glory, save in the cross of our Lord Jesus Christ, through which the world hath been crucified unto me." Gal. 6:14
5. I, crucified unto the world — "And I unto the world." Gal. 6:14

### Cross of Christ a Stumblingblock

1. To the Moralists — because works cannot justify.
2. To the Philosopher — because it appeals to faith, not reason.
3. To the Cultured — because its truth is revealed to babes.
4. To the High Caste — because God chose the poor and humble.
5. To the will — because it calls for unconditional surrender.

**I would that they were even cut off which troubleth you** (King James)

1. This verse has several translations.
2. Notice the differences:
a. *Cut off* in King James version.
b. One whole phrase is missing: "even go beyond circumcision."
3. The meaning is the same in both translations.
a. If these false teachers would be consistent, they would cut themselves off completely from the church.

b. Paul is saying: these troublers who mutilate the flesh, should go all the way and cut themselves off from the church.

### Study Questions 5:10-12

647. Do we see an indication that Paul is hopeful?
648. Has his earlier pessimism been changed or strengthened?
649. Will the mind of Christ offset the leaven of false doctrine?
650. Does the word "he" seem to infer that there was only one false teacher?
651. Could it refer to the devil?
652. Will the false one be punished?
653. Will we make the false teacher anathema or will God do it? Cf. II Cor. 10:6-8
654. Was Paul ever a preacher of circumcision?
655. Does this verse indicate that he had been falsely accused?
656. Could this be because he had Timothy circumcised?
657. How could false teachers preach circumcision and yet retain favor?
658. Are we to expect persecution when we preach truth?
659. How are we to face it?
660. Is the last part of the verse a question?
661. Does Paul teach elsewhere that the cross is a stumbling block?
662. If Paul preached both circumcision and the cross, would there have been less of a stumbling block?
663. Is Paul saying that the cancellation of the law by the cross is the stumbling block?
664. Compare translations on this verse. Do all of them mean the same?
665. Is Paul wishing that the false ones were dead?
666. How could they go beyond circumcision?
667. Does he infer that they ought to completely mutilate the flesh?
668. Does Paul mean that they ought to cut themselves off from the Church?

## B. LIMITATIONS AND POWER OF FREEDOM 5:13-26

1. No fleshly License 5:13-15

### Text 5:13-15

**13 For ye, brethren, were called for freedom; only use not your freedom for an occasion to the flesh, but through love be servants**

one to another.  14 For the whole law is fulfilled in one word,
even in this :Thou shalt love thy neighbor as thyself.   15 But if ye
bite and devour one another, take heed that ye be not consumed
one of another.

## Paraphrase

13 Now ye, brethren, have been called by the gospel into
freedom from the law of Moses as the rule of your justification.
Nevertheless, use not this liberty as a pretext for gratifying those
appetites, and exercising those passions, which have their seat in
the flesh. But, agreeably to the law of Christ, assiduously serve
one another in all things innocent.

14 They who stickle for the law ought to be zealous in the
offices of love. For the whole law, as it respects our neighbour,
is fulfilled by obeying one precept, even this: Thou shalt love
they neighbour as sincerely as thou lovest thyself.

15 But, if, from your zeal for, or your zeal against the law
of Moses, ye wound and destroy one another's characters, have
a care lest ye bring everlasting destruction on one another.

## Comment 5:13

### For ye, brethren

1. Paul called the Galatian Christian converts "brethren" even
   though he speaks strongly against their false teachers.
a. How long could they apostasize and be brethren?
b. Who among the sects, denominations, and divisions are our
   brethren?
c. How wrong must a Christian be to be out of the fellowship
   as a brother?
d. Is the follower of a false teacher a brother, while the false
   teacher is not to be considered so?
e. The problem of fellowship is not easily settled.
2. There are times when lines are to be drawn.
   "Anathema." Cf. Gal. 1:8-9
   "receive him not into your house." Cp. II John 1:10

### were called for freedom

1. A freedom from the burdensome rites and ceremonies of the
   law.  5:1
2. Freedom from the captivity of sin. Rom. 6:18
a. A Christian is the only free person.

b. God does not want us to be like Adam and Eve, hiding from him.
3. Freedom from death. Rom. 8:2

**only use not your freedom for an occasion to the flesh**

1. The devil would turn freedom to licentiousness.
a. The flesh reasons "If we are without the law, we may as well indulge."
b. "For there are certain men crept in privily, even they who were of old written of beforehand unto this condemnation, ungodly men, turning the grace of our God into lasciviousness." Jude 4
c. "Not using your freedom for a cloak of wickedness." I Peter 2:16
2. Freedom is not given for a person to act without restraint.

**but through love be servants one to another**

1. Folks want to be important; here is the way.
a. "Whosover would be first among you shall be your servant." Matt. 20:27
b. "But he that is greatest among you shall be your servant." Matt. 23:11
c. "Good and faithful servant . . . enter thou into the joy." Matt. 25:21
2. This is a debt.
"Owe no man anything, save to love one another." Rom. 13:8-10

## Comment 5:14

**For the whole law is fulfilled in one word, love** (Lev. 19:18)

1. People get worked up over ceremonies — rituals . When one word carefully carried out, is worth all the ritual possible.
a. Leave off all this foolishness and get down to business.
b. One thing will fulfill all the law—love.
2. This new commandment sounds "short and easy."
a. It is never accomplished—among men.
b. Loving wayward men is not easily accomplished.
c. Intolerance for sin is sometimes accompanied by intolerance for the sinner.

**as thyself**

1. You can't find a nearer example than yourself.

2. If you were in trouble you know how you would want to be treated.

## Comment 5:15

**but if ye bite and devour one another**

1. When the one faith in Christ is overthrown, peace and unity come to an end in the church.
a. Instead of being motivated by love, jealousy and strife prevail.
b. Backbiters are condemned by the Word: Rom. 1:30; Prov. 25:23; II Cor. 12:20
2. Falste teaching causes strife, etc. Cf. II Tim. 2:23, I Tim. 6:4

**take heed that ye be not consumed one of another**

1. Nothing is so destructive as religious disputes.
a. Both groups feel they are on God's side and the other is possessed of the devil.
b. Both have invested time and money and they do not want to see it turned to the enemy's advantage.
2. It consumes like a fire until Christians who are to give reasonable service become unreasonable.
3. The Church's greatest enemy is itself.

## Study Questions 5:13-15

669. Paul again emphasized freedom. Does he mean freedom from burdensome rites?
670. Were they in danger of misunderstanding freedom?
671. Do people tend to lawlessness if you free them from law?
672. Compare I Peter 2:16 on this subject.
673. Is freedom for people with restraint or without it?
674. What influence should restrain us?
675. If love is our motive what will a man do?
676. If a person breaks fellowship in acceptance of false teaching, is he serving his brethren in love?
677. What one law is worth more than all the rituals and ceremonies combined?
678. What one word fulfills all the law?
679. Did Christ fulfill the law?
680. Are you able to do it? Do you love your neighbors, friends, relatives, enemies?
681. Is intolerance for sin often accompanied by intolerance for sinners too?

147

682. Do you consider yourself a good example of how all men would like to be treated?
683. Is this commandment one of the ten commandments?
684. Is this commandment as easy as it is short?
685. Was Peter demonsrating the commandment when he severed fellowship?
686. Was Paul showing love when he withstood Peter face to face?
687. Does love require sterness as well as warmth?
688. How do people bite and devour without being cannibals?
689. Where is this spirit condemned?
690. Will the motive of love destroy this sin?
691. How consuming is a church fight?
692. Is the innocent party to be careful too?
693. Do you feel that a church may be its own worst enemy?

2. Victory over the flesh  5:16-26

## Text 5:16-18

**16 But I say, Walk by the Spirit, and ye shall not fulfill the lust of the flesh. 17 For the flesh lusteth against the Spirit, and the Spirit against the flesh; for these are contrary the one to the other; that ye may not do the things that ye would. 18 But if ye are led by the Spirit, ye are not under the law.**

### Paraphrase

16 I command then, Walk according to the dictates of your spiritual part, and so you will not gratify the lust of your animal nature; particularly, ye will not gratify the sinful passions of envy, malice, anger, revenge.

17 Ye have great need to subdue the lusts of the flesh: For the flesh strongly inclines men to act contrary to reason and conscience; and these principles are often contrary to one another, so that ye cannot always do the things which your better part inclines you to do. See Rom. 7:18.

18 But, to encourage you to subdue the flesh, know, that if ye habitually follow the dictates of your better part, ye are not under the curse of any law, so as to be punished.

### Comment 5:16

#### But I say, walk by the Spirit

1. MacKnight uses *spirit* to indicate man's spiritual part — the mind and conscience enlightened by the doctrines and precepts

148

of the gospel revealed by the Spirit.
2. Walking in the Spirit places one above carnal ordinances.

### ye shall not fulfill the lust of the flesh
1. Fulfill means to satisfy.
2. Satisfaction is the desire of the carnal man.
a. "the mind of the flesh is enmity against God." Rom. 8:7
b. "Ye ask, and receive not, because ye ask amiss, that ye may spend it in your pleasures." James 4:3

## Comment 5:17
### for the flesh lusteth against the Spirit
1. The definition of lust.
a. Unholy desire.
b. Unlawful desire.
2. The working of lust.
a. It burns. "Burned in their lusts one toward another." Rom. 1:27
b. It draws away. "Each man is tempted, when he is drawn away by his own lust, and enticed." James 1:14
c. It brings forth sin. "Then the lust when it hath conceived, beareth sin: and the sin, when it is full-grown bringeth forth death."
d. It is defilement. "But chiefly them that walk after the flesh in the lust of defilement and despite dominion." II Peter 2:10
e. It allures. "entice in the lusts." II Peter 2:18
3. The end of lust.
a. Passes away with the world. I John 2:17
b. Brings death. James 1:15

### and the Spirit against the flesh
1. These beastly traits God is against.
2. The Spirit seeks to constrain the flesh.

### these are contrary the one to the other
1. They do not attract, but repel.
2. Man's being is always locked in mortal combat.
3. A saint is not a piece of wood that has no feeling but is a combination that is in constant struggle.

### that ye may not do the things that ye would
1. Paul expresses it in Romans completely. See Rom. 7:15
2. The spiritual person is aware of the conflict within, while fleshly people do not care.

## Comment 5:18

**But if ye are led by the Spirit, ye are not under the law**

1. A wise person would select the Spirit in place of the lust.
a. No doubt law here refers to law of sin, not the Mosaic law.
b. It is used in connection with a discussion of sin.
2. Now if you make this wise choice, your choice frees you.

## Study Questions 5:16-18

694. Is this exhortation to produce fruit of Spirit?
695. How can a person walk in the Spirit when he walks in a world of flesh?
696. Can a person be so full of goodness that there is no room or time for evil.
697. Can you walk in the Spirit and walk with the devil's crowd?
698. What does the word *fulfill* mean? Will a man get ulcers frustrating the flesh?
699. How can a person have the mind of Christ instead of a carnal mind?
700. What does Paul mean by flesh?
701. Define the word "lust."
702. How do we know lawful desires and unlawful ones?
703. What is the end of lust?
704. Does he mean that the Spirit lusts too?
705. Define *contrary*.
706. Are men aware of this awful combat within them constantly?
707. Is the saint more conscious of the warfare than the worldly person?
708. Describe a life led by the Spirit?
709. If we are led by God's Spirit, are we leading our own lives?
710. What law is meant — law of Moses or of sin?

## Text 5:19,20

**19 Now the works of the flesh are manifest, which are these: fornication, uncleanness, lasciviousness, 20 idolatry, sorcery, enmities, strife, jealousies, wraths, factions, divisions, parties.**

## Paraphrase

19 Now, the works produced by the lust of the flesh are manifest: namely, adultery, fornication, and all kinds of uncleanness; such as incest, sodomy, bestiality, the indulging lascivious thoughts, and the reading of lascivious books;

20 The worshipping of idols, sorcery, or a pretended communication with the invisible malignant powers; enmities long kept up; quarrels issuing in unreasonable law-suits; ambitious emulations; violent anger; brawling; causeless separations; the forming of sects in religion, for the sake of gain, in opposition to conscience;

## Comment 5:19

Now the works of the flesh are manifest (order and expression differs in King James)

### Adultery

1. Illicit relationships with a married person — it ruins families, alienates children from parents and causes parents to neglect children.
2. This word is missing in some manuscripts: It is not in the American Standard.
3. In the Old Testament such a person was to be stoned to death. Lev. 20:10
4. Adultery will keep one out of heaven. I Cor. 6:9; Heb. 13:4
5. In Hollywood it seems to add to one's box office appeal.

### fornication

1. Illicit relationship of single or unmarried persons.
2. Fornicators will not be in heaven. Rev. 22:15
3. If adultery is not included in all Greek manuscripts, we may consider it included under fornication. See Matt. 5:32

### uncleanness

1. This word covers a wider range of sensual sin than fornication.
a. Eph. 4:19 speaks of "all uncleanness."
b. In Rom. 1:24 it refers to unnatural practices.
c. In II Cor. 12:21 it is connected with sexual perversion.
2. There are other sensual sins that must be included.
a. Tobacco is unclean.
1) It leaves a stain upon fingers that handle it.
2) It leaves a deposit in the lungs of the smokers.
3) It makes the breath smell unclean.
4) Wrappers, ashes, butts, litter streets and public houses.
5) It makes the clothes, the house, the car smell foul to the non-smoker.

6) Homes, cars, buses, banquet halls, and even some churches are made to smell from the smoke exhaled from the lungs.
b. Liquor is unclean.
1) Wherever men indulge there is vomit, men in gutters, automobile wrecks, blood and death.
2) It brings men to poverty and cheap, dirty hotels.

### lasciviousness

1. This word is also translated wantonness.
2. It comes from the Greek
a. The Pulpit Commentary: "It is scarcely an adequate translation in this connection. It appears to point to reckless shamelessness in unclean indulgences."
b. The Pulpit Commentary: "In classical Greek the adjective form describes a man insolently and wantonly reckless in his treatment of others, but in the N. T. it generally appears to point more specifically to unabashed open indulgences in impurity."
3. There are other uses of the word.
a. Used with uncleanness and fornication in II Cor. 12:21.
b. Used with uncleanness in Eph. 4:19.
c. Is used with men of Sodom in II Peter 2:7.
d. Compare II Peter 2:18; I Peter 4:3 and Jude 4.
4. In Mark 7:22 it may appear in its classical sense.

## Comment 5:20

### idolatry

1. The worshipping of idols could be considered a fruit of the flesh for pagan religions are lustful.
a. Temples have had their male and female prostitutes.
b. The most shameful practices have been done in the name of religion.
2. Paul warns about idolatry in I Cor. 8 and also 10.
3. Idolatry is not limited to pagan worship, but church members may be guilty.
a. "Put to death . . . covetousness, which is idolatry." Col. 3:5
b. "Stubbornness is as idolatry." I Sam. 15:22-23

### sorcery

1. This word is translated *witchcraft* in the King James version.
2. It is from the Greek word denoting the use of drugs, but this

sense is not used here.

3. The word in some forms was often used in reference to the employment of drugs in charms and incantations.
4. This sin is in bad company.
   a. "murders . . . sorceries . . . fornication." Rev. 9:21; 21:8; 22:15
   b. The sorcerers and magicians of Egypt. Exodus 7:11
   c. Magical books. Acts 19:19
   d. Imposters. II Tim. 3:13
5. Art Baker on a television program in February 1951, had a spiritualist expose the work of mediums and announce that Americans pay $125,000,000 annually for this deceit.

### enmities

1. This is translated *hatred* in the King James.
2. Differences over issues and differences in the churches sometimes make enemies out of brethren.
3. Brethren should have love rather than hatred in their hearts.
4. How can the church member condemn Russia if he has enmity within his heart for those in the church?

### strife

1. This is translated *variance* in the King James.
2. This is the outward conflict of persons.
3. When hatred goes to work and appears in the open it is strife.
   a. "Hatred stirreth up strifes." Prov. 10:12
   b. "A wrathful man stirreth up contention." Prov. 15:18
4. Strife comes from other sources than hatred.
   "A proud heart stirreth up strife." Prov. 28:25
   Strife gendered between herdsmen. Gen. 13:7
   Strife arose among disciples over greatness. Luke 22:24
   Carnality causes strife. I Cor. 3:3
   False teaching causes strife. I Tim. 6:4
   Foolish questions gender strife. II Tim. 2:23

### jealousies

1. *Emulations* is the translation of the King James.
   a. The meaning is "ambitious" or "envious rivalry."
   b. In this case it has the idea of resentment.
2. In the original Greek it has the idea of "zeal."
   a. Zeal is good until corrupted.

b. Most vices are corrupted virtues.

3. The word is often connected with strife.
"Not in strife and jealousy." Rom. 13:13
"Among you jealousy and strife." I Cor. 3:3
"I fear . . . I should find . . . strife, jealousy." II Cor. 12:20

**wrath**

1. Wrath here is uncontrolled anger—passionate—probably with physical harm in mind.

2. Self control is a requirement for an elder.
"The bishop must be . . . no brawler." I Tim. 3:3
"Not to be contentious." Titus 3:2

3. Wrath or anger has its place if controlled.
"Be ye angry, and sin not." Eph. 4:26
"O ye that love Jehovah, hate evil." Ps. 97:10

a. This does not mean that we should be hateful to those who are sinful.

b. See Matt. 5:44-48.

**factions**

1. The Pulpit Commentary challenges this word being translated strife as it appears in the King James.

a. The verb from which it is derived means to act the part of a day-labourer, then scheming or intriguing for a post of employment.

b. Next, it means "party action" — the contentious spirit of faction.

2. There are six other passages where the word appears.

a. "Unto them that are factious." Rom. 2:8

b. "Some indeed preach Christ even of envy and strife." Phil. 1:15

c. "Doing nothing through faction." Phil. 2:3

d. See also II Cor. 12:20 and James 3:14-16.

3. In writing to Titus, Paul gives a warning about such people. Titus 3:10

a. "A factious man after a first and second admonition refuse." Titus 3:10

b. This word here is translated *heretic* in the King James, but appears as *factious* in the American Standard.

**divisions**

1. *Seditions* is the King James translation.
a. Sedition means "going aside."
b. It carries the idea of insurrection, tending to excite, arousing to the point of going aside.
2. This is, distinctly formed parties standing apart from each other.
a. Division is the result of carnality. I Cor. 3:3-5
b. Divisions indicate a lack of perfection. I Cor. 1:10
3. The Lord's way is oneness, for that is the content of His prayer in John 17.

**parties.**

1. The King James translates this word *heresies.*
2. The word in the original had the idea of "choice of views."
3. The Pulpit Commentary has a thorough discussion of this word.
a. The gospel is a revelation, it is not an opinion.
b. Opinions about the gospel makes heresies or parties.

## Study Questions 5:19,20

711. Why does he use the word "works" in connection with the flesh?
712. Is this the word used when he speaks of the spiritual life?
713. What is the difference in works and fruit?
714. Define adultery.
715. What was the penalty for it in the Old Testament?
716. What is the penalty for it in Hollywood?
717. Can we get to heaven and be guilty of adultery?
718. Define fornication.
719. Are guilty ones to be included in heaven?
720. Can we be guilty even though we do not commit it in the flesh, according to Jesus?
721. If filthy literature is read and suggestive shows are seen, are we guilty?
722. Define uncleanness.
723. Is this limited to a failure to bathe?
724. What common sins could be classed as sensual?
725. Is it limited to sexual perversion?
726. Are dirty habits to be included in the category of uncleanness?

727. Define lasciviousness.
728. What kind of company does it keep?
729. Are people proud of their impurity?
730. Do night club entertainers capitalize on this sin?
731. Can you be guilty and be saved?
732. Should Christians today be warned against idolatry?
733. Did Paul warn us against it?
734. What was Paul's definition of it?
735. Could church members be guilty of it?
736. Is a stingy church an idolatrous one?
737. Define sorcery.
738. What other terms are used in various translations?
739. Is it in bad company, according to other scriptures?
740. Is its use limited to heathen witch-doctors?
741. Define enmities.
742. Can the church condemn politics in Russia if it is guilty of enmity?
743. Does your congregation have any enmity in it?
744. Define strife.
745. What are its sources?
746. Could false teaching be guilty?
747. Are denominations striving against one another?
748. Is it better to have silent enmity than outward conflict?
749. Define jealousy.
750. Is it a corrupted zeal?
751. Were Christ's apostles guilty?
752. Are musicians, teachers, etc., in the church guilty of this sin?
753. Define wrath.
754. Is it wrong to have anger?
755. How can we have anger, and sin not?
756. Find verses that condemn angry outburst.
757. Define wrath.
758. Is God a God of wrath?
759. Can a person have controlled anger?
760. Is this sin sufficient to disqualify an elder?
761. What does wrath lead to?
762. Explain the value of anger.
763. Define factions.

764. Is it a common sin?
765. How many times does the Bible condemn it?
766. Are we to be patient and longsuffering with the factious man?
767. How do we know when we are dealing with such a person?
768. Define *divisions* as used in the New Testament.
769. Did the Corinthian church have this problem?
770. What was Paul's condemnation for it?
771. If it was wrong to name the church and thus divide it then, how about naming the church after men today?
772. Is denominationalism the same as divisions?
773. Is it against Christ's prayer for oneness?
774. What does the New Testament mean by *oneness?*
775. What does the New Testament mean by parties?
776. Do we have the right to a choice of views?
777. Is modernism a choice between God's view and man's views?
778. Do opinions versus revelation make parties?

## Text 5:21

**21 envyings, drunkenness, revellings, and such like; of which I forewarn you, even as I did forewarn you, that they who practice such things shall not inherit the kingdom of God.**

## Paraphrase

21 Inward grievings at the happiness of others; the taking of men's lives unjustly, and the maiming of their members; drinkings to intoxication; lewd frolics, and running through the streets in the night-time; and such like evil practices: concerning which I foretell you now, as I have often done formerly, that they who practice such things shall not inherit the kingdom of God. Awful declaration!

## Comment 5:21

**Envyings**
1. When you feel a pain at the sight or sound of excellence or happiness you are envious.
a. Are you able to enjoy the success, the victories, and joys of other people?
b. There is no room for envy in a Christian's life, nor in the church.
2. What is the difference between envy and jealousy?
a. Envy—One who discontentedly desires or covets the good fortunes or attainments of others is envious.

b. Jealousy—One is jealous who suspects and resents the diversion to another (especially to one regarded as a rival) of what one loves or prizes as his own.

3. The scriptures speak on the subject.

a. Examples of envy.

1) "Jews, were filled with jealousy." Acts 13:45

2) "Jews being moved with jealousy." Acts 17:5

3) The Philistines envied Isaac. Gen. 26:14

4) "Rachel envied her sister." Gen. 30:1

5) Joseph's brothers envied him. Gen. 37:11

b. Condemnation of it.

1) "Putting away . . . envies." I Peter 2:1

2) ". . . Love envieth not . . ." I Cor. 13:4

3) See also James 3:14-16.

### murder

1. This word does not appear in the American Standard version.

a. It definitely is a fruit of the flesh.

b. Some felt that the Galatians were not guilty of this sin, that the others were appropriate to them.

2. Murder is not alone the taking of life.

a. Hear Jesus — "For out of the heart come forth evil thoughts, murders, adulteries, etc." Matt. 5:19

b. Hear John — "Whosoever hateth his brother is a murderer." I John 3:15

### drunkenness

1. Millions are spent on liquor in face of the warning that drunkards will be condemned. I Cor. 6:10

2. Liquor is the greatest enemy to marriage, yet America spends a large percentage of its income on liquor.

a. Divorce is the Number One cause of juvenile delinquency — yet America drinks.

b. This is an awful price for freedom in appetites.

### revellings

1. "Revelling" is carrying to excess such things as feasting, drinking, and hilarity.

a. Sin fills the night air with jesting, carousing, etc.

b. It is to take great or intense delight or satisfaction in merrymaking.

2. This may have been a special sin of people in this area, for Peter likewise writes to the churches of "Pontus, Galatia—" saying: "lust, winebibbing, revellings, carousings, and . . . excess of riot . . ." I Peter 4:3-4

**and such like**

1. He has not named everything specifically but he has given examples, and anything like them are just as much condemned.
a. "Such like" means works which are like these.
b. He has not named the theatre, gambling or dancing, but they are "such like."
2. These sins may be placed in categories.
a. Sin against marriage is adultery and fornication, the seventh commandment.
b. Sin against the dignity of the body is uncleanness, lasciviousness, drunkenness, and revelry.
c. Sin against the first and second commandment is idolatry, or witchcraft.
d. Sin against a neighbor is hatred, variance, wrath.
e. Sin against the church is heresies, factions.
f. Sin against one's mind is envy, jealousy.

**shall not inherit the kingdom of God**

1. What will they inherit?
a. "Their part shall be in the lake of fire . . ." Rev. 21:8
b. "For without are the dogs . . ." Rev. 22:15
2. *The kingdom of God* is a familiar expression.
"Worthy of the kingdom of God." II Thess. 1:5
"His heavenly kingdom." II Tim. 4:18
"Entrance into the eternal kingdom." II Peter 1:11

## Study Questions 5:21

779. Define envy.
780. Compare it to jealousy.
781. Give Biblical examples of envy.
782. Is it a common sin today?
783. How strongly is it condemned in the Bible?
784. Does love envy?
785. Define the word "murder."
786. How serious are murderous thoughts according to Jesus?

787. Would your church be shocked if all murderous thoughts were revealed as in a newspaper?

788. Define drunkenness.

789. Does Paul say that this is only a disease?

790. If an alcoholic is a drunkard because he has alcoholic disease can God condemn him?

791. Are people who vote for liquor guilty of helping to make drunkards?

792. Is the United States a drunkard nation?

793. How much was the liquor bill for the last political election?

794. Have you heard where in the United States the most liquor is consumed per capita?

795. Define revellings.

796. What cities are known for their all night gambling and drinking dens?

797. Is all merry-making revelling?

798. How far can one go in fun without being guilty?

799. How much money is spent in the United States on revelling?

800. Define "such like."

801. What all would you include in this category?

802. What if someone prepares a list with which you disagree?

803. Should we speak with the same authority about the ones we name as the ones specifically stated in the Word?

804. Is your preacher a hobbyist on the "such like" subjects or does he prefer to speak where the Word speaks?

805. If these flesh workers do not inherit the kingdom of God what will they inherit?

806. What is the kingdom of God?

807. Why will men take their chances on the two kingdoms?

## Text 5:22,23

**22 But the fruit of the Spirit is love, joy, peace, long-suffering, kindness, goodness, faithfulness, 23 meekness, self-control; against such there is no law.**

## Paraphrase

22 But the fruit which reason enlightened by the Spirit of God produceth, is love to God and man; joy, occasioned by that excellent affection; peace with all men; the patient bearing of injuries; a soft and sweet manner of speaking; a beneficent dis-

position; fidelity in engagements, promises, and trust;

23 Calmness under provocations; temperance in the use of meats and drinks. In praise of these virtues I observe, that there never was any law or religion by which they were prohibited, or the persons punished who practiced them.

## Comment 5:22

### Fruit

1. The word "fruit" here takes the place of "works" in verse 19.
a. Trees that produce fruit are cultivated on the account of the fruit.
b. Glorious things in our lives will be produced as fruit, if we choose to be spiritual.
2. Fruit is a proof of the tree.
a. "For the tree is known by its fruit." Matt. 12:33
b. "A good tree cannot bring forth evil fruit." Matt. 7:18
3. The source of good fruit is described.
a. "Fruit of the Spirit." Gal. 5:22
b. "The gospel . . . is bearing . . . fruit in you." Col. 1:6
c. "He that abideth in me . . . beareth much fruit." Jn. 15:5
4. The ways that we bear fruit are listed.
"let us offer fruit of lips that make confession to his name." Heb. 13:15
"this shall bring fruit from my work." Phil. 1:22
"The fruit of righteousness is sown in peace . . ." James 3:18
"Bring forth fruit with patience." Luke 8:15
By being cleansed. John 15:2
"Abiding in Christ." John 15:5

### of the Spirit

1. Is the word *spirit* here, the spirit of man or the Holy Spirit?
a. Commentators do not seem anxious to deal with the question.
b. The word is capitalized in the Scripture which expresses the viewpoint of the majority of scholars involved in translation.
c. MacKnight says "It is not possible to give a higher praise to any temper of mind or course of life than to say it is the fruit of the Spirit; whether by the spirit we understand the Spirit of God, or the spirit of man."
d. The Pulpit Commentary says: "The relation expressed here by the genitive case of the noun, 'of the Spirit' is probably

much the same as is expressed by the corresponding genitive, 'of the flesh,' in each case meaning 'belonging to' or 'due to the operation of'; for the agent who in the one case does the works is not the flesh, but the person acting under the influence of the flesh; so here the fruitbearer is not 'the Spirit, but the person controlled by the Spirit.' "

2. An examination of life, of history, and of scripture reveals that man is sinful, so these fruits are not the fruits of man's spirit. The fruits of Gal. 5:22-23 are Divine attributes.

a. However, these fruits do not appear in our lives without strenuous endeavor on our part.

b. "Work out your own salvation with fear and trembling." Phil. 2:12-13

### Love

1. Much has been said on the subject but none is so eloquent as I Cor. 13.

2. Jesus must be heard, for He says that love is in three directions: toward God, toward man, and toward self. Matt. 22:37

a. Love toward men is in two directions: toward those that love us, and toward our enemies.

1) "Love your enemies." Matt. 5:44

2) There is no honor in loving those that love you. Matt. 5:46

b. Love will prove our discipleship.
"By this shall all men know . . ." John 13:35

3. John should be heard—for he speaks so pointedly.

a. "If a man say, I love God, and hateth his brother, he is a liar: for he that loveth not his brother whom he hath seen, cannot love God whom he hath not seen." I John 4:20

b. "God is love; and he that abideth in love, abideth in God." I John 4:16

### joy

1. This is radiance, a bubbling forth, like a mountain spring that has an eternal source.

a. There is no room for complaint of one's portion.

b. Listen to Paul in prison—in need of cloak, and parchments.

1) "Finally my brethren, rejoice in the Lord." Phil. 3:1

2) "Rejoice in the Lord always: again I will say, Rejoice." Phil. 4:4

3) "I know how to be abased, and I know also how to abound." Phil. 4:12
c. Hear Paul in writing to Romans: "for the kingdom of God is not eating and drinking, but righteousness and peace and joy in the Holy Spirit." Rom. 14:17

2. The contrast would be the coldness and severity of feeling which many people have.

a. The Christian can not testify of the blessedness of Christ if his face is long, and his stories of hardship are endless.

b. Let us radiate joy and happiness until the world will desire the Christ.

**peace**

1. Two things definitely will be absent from the heart that has peace.

a. Worry will be absent: "Be not anxious for your life." Matt. 6:25

b. Hatred and strife will be absent.

1) Abraham said, "Let there be no strife." Gen. 13:8

2) "on earth, peace, among men." Luke 2:14

3) "the mind of the Spirit is peace . . ." Rom. 8:6

4) "He is our peace." Eph. 2:14

2. Peace proves our wisdom: "The wisdom that is from above is first pure, then peaceable." James 3:17

3. This virtue practiced would end all war: "That we may lead a quiet and peaceful (*tranquil* A.S.) life." I Tim. 2:2

**longsuffering**

1. Paul expresses this is as a result of love: "love suffereth long." I Cor. 13:4

a. What is wrong, but a lack of love, when marriages do not last a year?

b. Love is not present when some churches have folks sitting on opposite sides of the building to keep from speaking to each other.

c. Men are quick to cease their efforts for good.

2. God is longsuffering; without this grace there would be no salvation.

a. "Longsuffering—not wishing that any should perish." II Peter 3:9

b. "Longusffering . . . in the days of Noah." I Peter 3:20
c. Men would blow the universe up in disgust, but God waits.

### kindness

1. This, in the King James, is *gentleness*.
2. The etymology of the word means "usableness" and seems to suggest sweetness of disposition, a willingness to comply, a willingness to be of service to others.
3. This word in the Greek appears in II Cor. 6:6; Eph. 2:7; Col. 3:1; Titus 3:4, and is translated as *kindness*.
4. In Rom. 2:4—The same word is translated *goodness*.
5. Paul in I Cor. 13:4 speaks of love being kind; so if we will love, many good things will result.
a. Courtesy, sympathy, and understanding are in the word *kind*.
b. Consideration will be an attribute of one who is kind.
6. One who is kind will watch his speech, for words can cut deeply and wound severely the sensitive soul.

### goodness

1. This term seems to be a wide art of benevolence. See Rom. 5:14, also Eph. 5:9
2. The Christian is to be more than good; his life is to be exceedingly good, as Jesus expressed in Matt. 5:20
3. It is to be exercised especially toward the Christian. Gal. 6:10

### faithfulness

1. There seems to be some dispute as to what shade of meaning the apostle had—faith or faithfulness.
a. The Pulpit Commentary insists that the idea of fidelity, which the word bears in Titus 2:10, seems out of place when we consider the particular evils which are now in his eye as existing or in danger of arising in the Galatian Church.
b. The Commentary says "belief in the gospel fits the occasion perfectly."
2. It would be a rare case that a lesson on faithfulness would not be needed.
3. If Christ is unchanging (Heb. 13:8), then faithfulness must be included in the list of the fruit of the Spirit.
4. It is essential to salvation.
a. "Be thou faithful unto death." Rev. 2:10
b. "Except ye believed in vain." I Cor. 15:2

c. "Endureth to the end." Matt. 10:22

d. "No man . . . looking back . . . is fit." Luke 9:62

## Comment 5:23

**meekness**

1. This is quite often thought of as weakness, but the two words resemble each other only in sound.

a. It does not mean spiritless but does mean the opposite of domineering and blustering.

b. It means mild of temper, patient under injuries.

2. There is strength in humility.

a. Moses was meek. Numbers 12:3

b. Jesus was meek. Matt. 11:29

c. Now, name two men who had a greater influence for human society than these two persons.

3. Examine the words of Jesus in the light of history: "The meek shall inherit the earth." Matt. 5:5 Cf. Ps. 37:11

a. Hitler with his "goose step" and brag of a superior race, went down to defeat, to poverty, to ashes, and destruction.

b. Those nations that allow the meek and lowly Jesus to be preached, are the leading nations of the world.

c. If our riches destroy our meekness then "pride goeth before destruction." Prov. 16:18

4. There are some very fine instructions on the subject.

a. "In meekness correcting." II Tim. 2:25

b. "Walk . . . with lowliness and meekness." Eph. 4:2

c. "Showing all meekness." Titus 3:2

d. "Receive with meekness." James 1:21

e. "Give a reason . . . concerning hope . . . with meekness." I Peter 3:15

**self control**

1. *Temperance* is the King James translation.

2. This word stands in opposition to such words as fornication, drunkenness, and revellings, named in the chapter.

3. Control of mind and body is an essential for an elder. See I Tim. 3:2-4; also Titus 2:2.

4. Alexander the Great controlled the world at age 33, but died at that age because he failed to control his own lusts.

**against such there is no law**

1. These attributes are generally recognized as beneficial, hence men do not legislate against them.

a. Who would want a law against being kind? Humane societies are formed to encourage men to extend kindness to animals.

b. These are opposed by the law of lust, but no legislation of man or God is against the fruit of the Spirit.

2. The law of Moses is not against these.

a. The law could not produce righteousness. Gal. 3:21

b. We walk not after the flesh. See Rom. 8:4.

c. The law pointed out these sins, so the law would not be against these.

## Study Questions 5:22,23

808. What does the Spirit produce — fruit or works?

809. Is fruit a proof of the kind of a tree?

810. Is the Spirit the source of good fruit?

811. Find as many places in God's Word as you can where the word fruit is used.

812. Is the word *Spirit* capitalized?

813. Does this indicate man's fruit or God's fruit?

814. Are they divine attributes even though you should conclude that the word *spirit* is used here to be opposite flesh?

815. Why does he put *love* first here, when he places it last in I Cor. 13:13?

816. Should love be first, last, and always?

817. What love is meant in this verse?

818. Does he mean love for God or love for man, or both?

819. What if we do not have love in our heart?

820. Describe joy.

821. Can one be sour, disgruntled, and a chronic complainer and be joyful?

822. When should be person be joyful?

823. Where may we exhibit joy as a testimony of our faith?

824. If Christians were joyful, would it be a contrast to the fun-loving world?

825. Describe peace.

826. If one has worry and anxiety, does he have peace?

827. Is the peace described here only the absence of war?

828. How are peace and wisdom connected?

829. What will be absent from the heart of the man who is peaceful?

830. Define longsuffering.

831. In what relationship should longsuffering work?

832. Is God longsuffering toward us?

833. Define kindness.

834. What does Paul say about it in I Cor. 13?

835. Can you hate and be kind?

836. Can you love and be unkind?

837. Do people in love sometime treat others with more kindness than they do each other?

838. Do we take advantage of the longsuffering of others?

839. How can unkindness manifest itself?

840. Are you able to define goodness?

841. Is it easier to define than it is to practice?

842. Are we to be as good as the Pharisees?

843. Define faithfulness.

844. Are faith and faithfulness the same?

845. Is God faithful? What is the evidence?

846. Is faithfulness essential to salvation?

847. When a person lacks it, has he fallen from grace?

848. If your answer to the two former questions is yes, then is it possible for a person to fall from grace and to be lost?

849. Define meekness in the Word of God.

850. Is it weakness or does it have strength?

851. Jesus said that the meek would inherit the earth: in the light of Communistic power does He seem to be right?

852. Give examples of great people who were meek.

853. Name some other scriptures that teach on the subject of meekness.

854. Explain the meaning of self control.

855. How do other translations speak of it?

856. What appetites destroy control?

857. Is a failure at this point enough to disqualify a man for the eldership?

858. Have you heard of laws against these virtues?

859. Why do men not legislate against kindness, love, patience, etc.?

860. What kind of a world would we have if all our society produced the fruit of the Spirit?

## Text 5:24-26

**24 And they that are of Christ Jesus have crucified the flesh with the passions and the lusts thereof. 25 If we live by the Spirit, by the Spirit let us also walk. 26 Let us not become vainglorious, provoking one another, envying one another.**

## Paraphrase

24 Besides, they who are Christ's brethren, have from love to him, and admiration of his character, crucified the body with the passions and lusts proper to it.

25 Since we live in the spiritual dispensation of the gospel, and enjoy the spiritual gifts, let us also walk by the spirit; that is, by the rules prescribed in this spiritual dispensation.

26 In particular, let us who enjoy the spiritual gifts, beware of being puffed up with pride, lest we provoke one another to anger; and let us who want these gifts, abstain from envying those who possess them.

## Comment 5:24

**they that are of Christ Jesus**

1. *Christ Jesus* is not a common expression.
a. It occurs in Eph. 3:1 and Col. 2:6.
b. The title *Christ* means the "Anointed one," so it is "The Anointed Jesus."
c. It is questioned whether the expression is descriptive or a proper name.
2. The expression is one of possession: "are of Christ Jesus."
a. We, as Christians, are Christ's; we belong to Him.
"Ye are Christ's . . ." I Cor. 3:23
"We are the Lord's." Rom. 14:8
"God's own possession." Eph. 1:14
3. How do we become possessed of God and Christ?
a. By faith we recognize Him as Lord.
b. By repentance we will to become like Him.
c. By baptism we die to the past and rise to walk in the kingdom of Christ.

d. Our life is then a confession, accompanied by the words of our lips, that we are His.

e. Rom. 8:15 tells us that we may know that we are His.

1) The Spirit's testimony says believe, confess, repent, be baptized, be faithful.

2) My spirit says I have done these; therefore, the Spirit's testimony and my testimony are in accord.

3) We are none of His if we have not been obedient.

f. "As many as are led by the Spirit . . . these are sons of God." Rom. 8:14

**have crucified the flesh with the passions and the lusts thereof**

1. This crucifixion is best described by Rom. 6:1-6

a. Crucifixion is accomplished at baptism when one has willed to die to sin.

1) There is nothing magical about water, that can conquer sin.

2) Baptism crucifies only when mentally and spiritually there is a death to sin and a birth of the Spirit.

b. Our "old man" is crucified with Him.

1) We hang the flesh on the cross of Jesus.

2) The flesh must not be taken down to ourselves again.

2. What is the difference between passions and lusts?

a. Passion appears as *affections* in the King James version.

b. The Pulpit Commentary says:

1) *Passions* (affections) denotes the disordered states of the soul viewed as in a condition of a disease.

2) *Lusts* points to the goings forth of the soul towards objects which it is wrong to pursue.

c. MacKnight says *passions* are malice, anger, revenge, envy, and pride.

## Comment 5:25

**If we live by the Spirit, by the Spirit let us also walk.**

1. This suggests the sphere in which we should walk.

a. "Ye are not in the flesh but in the Spirit, if so be that the Spirit of God dwelleth in you." Rom. 8:9

b. It is a spiritual realm rather than a physical one.

2. At least three things will manifest themselves in a Spirit Walk.

a. In the production of the fruit of the Spirit.

b. In soul winning.

"... they had been with Jesus." Acts 4:13

"... turned world upside down. . ." Acts 17:6

c. In worship. Acts 2:42

## Comment 5:26

**let us not**

1. This is a communicative form of exhortation in which the exhorter joins himself with the ones being exhorted.

a. Why? Perhaps to soften the tone of superiority implied in exhorting them.

b. A second viewpoint is to imply that they as yet were not vainglorious but were in danger of becoming so.

c. A third definitely should be stated, "for this was a temptation that could befall anyone including Paul."

**become vainglorious**

1. *Vainglorious* means empty glory; perhaps a vain thinking respecting one's self.

2. Gal. 6:3 probably throws light on what Paul means: "If a man thinketh himself to be something when he is nothing, he deceiveth himself."

3. Boasting of one's attainment or even puffing up one's own self to oneself would be destructive of spiritual life.

**provoking one another**

1. This word is found nowhere else in the N.T.

2. *Provoking*, says the Pulpit Commentary, is perhaps not meant in the sense in which this English verb is now commonly used, as making angry, but challenging to legal controversy, or to battle, or to mutual comparative estimation in any way.

3. There is a good provocation. "Provoke . . . unto love and good works." Heb. 10:24

**envying one another**

1. There is a definite correlation of these two words, both of which appear only here in the N. T. (Pulpit Commentary).

a. One group who thought they were strong, would challenge; another group who found themselves weaker, would enevy.

b. Both faults are traced to one root—the excessive wish to be thought much of.

## Study Questions 5:24-26

861. Is the order of Jesus' names unusual here?
862. What does each title mean?
863. Does this indicate that some belong to Christ?
864. How do we become possessed by Christ?
865. How do we know when we are?
866. When does one crucify the flesh?
867. When flesh is crucified, what goes with it?
868. Does the water crucify the flesh?
869. What is the difference between passions and lusts?
870. Where in Romans is this subject discussed?
871. With whom are we crucified?
872. Is the Christian to consider himself fleshly or spiritual?
873. What characterizes a spiritual walk?
874. How can we allow the Spirit to lead our walk?
875. If we live by the Spirit, would our walk naturally be a spiritual walk?
876. Did Paul include himself in this exhortation?
877. Does this imply that the Galatians were not yet guilty of vanity?
878. Define vainglories.
879. Is the proud person an empty person?
880. What is meant by provoking one another?
881. Is provocation good or bad, or both?
882. What right have Christian people to envy one another?
883. What is basically wrong with the individual who is envious?

## Questions on Galatians, Chapter Five

### Completion:

1. For freedom did _____ set us free.
2. I Paul say unto you, that if ye receive _____ Christ will profit you nothing.
3. Every man that accepts circumcision, is a _____ to do the whole law.
4. Ye who are justified by the law are fallen away from

_____ .

5. Walk by the _____ and ye shall not fulfill the lust of the flesh.

6. If ye are led by the Spirit, ye are not under the _____.
7. The flesh lusteth against the _____.
8. A little leaven leaveneth the whole _____.
9. If ye be circumcised Christ shall profit you _____.
10. They that are Christ's have _____ the flesh with the affections and lusts.
11. The Galatians were told this _____ cometh not of him that calleth you.
12. We through the _____ wait for the hope of righteousness by faith.
13. Paul warned the Galatians about being entangled again in a yoke of _____.
14. Paul names the fruit of the Spirit and says, against such there is no _____.
15. Paul says "ye were running well, who _____ you that ye should not obey the truth".

### True - False

_____ 1. According to Paul it is possible to be severed from Christ.
_____ 2. Paul warns that freedom must not be used as an occasion for the flesh.
_____ 3. Paul states that the fulfillment of the law is "Thou shalt love thy neighbor as thyself."
_____ 4. Paul enumerates the fruit of the Spirit and then follows it with a catalogue of the fruits of the flesh.
_____ 5. Factions and divisions are named as works of the flesh along with drunkenness and revellings.

## Special Study On The Spirit Filled Life

### Man and the Spirit — Three actions of the Spirit

I. Walk in the Spirit
"I say walk by the Spirit and ye shall not fulfill the lust of the flesh." Gal. 5:16
A. A person's walk speaks a lot.
1. Walk of the timid, shy.
2. Walk of the arrogant.
3. Walk of the thief.
4. Walk of the kind.
5. Walk of the sorrowing.
6. Walk of the joyful.
7. Walk of the conqured, vanquished.

8. Walk of the Victorian.

B. Where a person walks, is an index to his character.
1. To sports.
2. To taverns.
3. To the needy.
4. To Church.

C. Walk in the Spirit and you will be kept away from the walk in sin.

II. Be led of the Spirit — "If ye are led by the Spirit, ye are not under the law." Gal. 5:18

A. The majority of people are led, not leaders.
1. Led into sin — drinking — gambling.
2. Led into crime.
3. The world is full of Judases who betray.
a) Judas — Goat who leads sheep to slaughter.

B. Majority are led by laws — they do not make them.
1. Illustration in national life.
2. Illustration in moral realm.
a) Bow to sin — under its power — its law.
b) Subject to a power beyond their own.

C. We have a leader who will help us to escape bondage.
1. "He leadeth me beside still waters." Psalm 23
2. The Holy Spirit leads us into all truth — The Bible.

III. Live in the Spirit — "If we live by the Spirit, by the Spirit let us also walk." Gal. 5:25

A. It is the right way. John 14:6

B. It is the eternal way.
1. Live any other way — and your experience is death.
2. "Soweth to the flesh . . . reap corruption." Gal. 6:8

C. It is the satisfying way.
1. Sin brings regret — bondage — death.
2. The Spirit gives life — peace.

**Conclusion: Take Your Choice.**

A. Walk by the leading of the Spirit and you will live.

B. Walk by the leading of Sin and you will die.

173

## C. DEMAND OF FREEDOM 6:1-10

### 1.  Mutual helpfulness and responsibilities 6:1-5

#### Text 6:1-5

**1 Brethren, even if a man be overtaken in any trespass, ye who are spiritual, restore such a one in a spirit of gentleness; looking to thyself, lest thou also be tempted. 2 Bear ye one another's burdens, and so fulfill the law of Christ. 3 For if a man thinketh himself to be something when he is nothing, he deceiveth himself. 4 But let each man prove his own work, and then shall he have his glorying in regard of himself alone, and not of his neighbor. 5 For each man shall bear his own burden.**

#### Paraphrase

1 Also, brethren, if any member of your churches, through the strength of temptation, or the frailty of his own nature, is surprised into any work of the flesh, ye who are teachers and rulers, restore such a person to his proper place in Christ's body, the church, by meek instructions and affectionate rebukes; and thou who readest, take a view of thine own frailty, lest even thou fall by temptation.

2 Instead of rebuking one another with harshness, sympathize with one another in every distress; and thus fulfill the law of Christ, which enjoins benevolence even to those who fall into sin.

3 For if any one, thinking highly of himself, is immoderately severe towards his brethren when they fall into sin, and does not assist the distressed, such a person, being nothing, deceiveth himself in thinking himself better than others.

4 But, the worth of a man being shewn by his works, let every one try his own work, rather than the work of others, and if good, then he shall have boasting in himself alone, and not in another, as worse than him.

5 To bring your actions to the trial, is absolutely necessary; for every one, at the judgment, shall answer for his own actions only.

#### Comment 6:1

**Brethren, even if a man be overtaken in any trespass**

1. The King James uses the word *fault.*
2. Many folk have a besetting sin that overtakes them on occasion.
3. Consider the word *overtaken.*

a. The devil can overtake — overcome in life as well as in doctrine.

b. "That they may recover themselves out of the snare of the devil, having been taken captive by him unto his will." II Tim. 2:26

c. This is not willful sin — but one whose spiritual endurance is at an end.

4. The Galatians are addressed as brethren.

a. Paul calls attention to a family relationship which should serve to obligate one to the needy.

b. God's family relationship should warm our hearts toward those in need.

## ye who are spiritual

1. Some feel these were men among the Galatians who were eminet for their knowledge and goodness.

2. MacKnight thinks they were those possessed of spiritual gifts. "If any man thinketh himself to be . . . spiritual." I Cor. 14:37

## restore such a one

1. Not to aggravate, scold, and drive further away.

a. The Greek word means "To make fit."

b. It is used in Matt. 4:21 of repairing nets.

c. Lidell and Scott says it is used of setting a broken limb.

2. What if he will not be restored?

a. Paul answers, "Refuse him." Titus 3:10

3. There is a state beyond restoration.

a. "Impossible to renew." Heb. 6:4-6

## in a spirit of gentleness

1. A repentant sinner is not to be given gall and vinegar to drink.

2. "Shall I come to you with a rod, or in love and a spirit of gentleness?" I Cor. 4:21

## looking to thyself

1. There is no sin which one person has committed, but what another may commit it.

2. We can examine others and forget self.

a. "But I buffet my body, and bring it into bondage: lest by any means, after that I have preached to others, I myself should be rejected." I Cor. 9:27

b. "Wherefore let him that thinketh he standeth take heed lest he fall." I Cor. 10:12

1) David fell.

2) Noah, a preacher of righteousness, fell.

3. Preachers can get so negative that they become sour and disgruntled.

a. Some men preach that others need to pray and to love, and they do not realize that they need it.

b. Some men preach as though they were the only saints.

4. Preachers can emphasize love and be unlovely.

5. *Looking* is also translated *considering*.

a. The verb denotes looking intently — being on guard.

1) "Look therefore whether the light that is in thee be not darkness." Luke 11:35

2) "Mark them that are causing the divisions." Rom. 16:17

b. Sometimes it is used as something to aim at.

1) "While we look not at the things which are seen." II Cor. 4:18

2) "Not looking each of you to his own things, but each of you also to the things of others." Phil. 2:4

**lest thou also be tempted**

1. He fell yesterday, I may fall today.

2. The restoring one may fall short of his duty.

a. He may withhold help.

b. He may be betrayed into Pharisaism — self righteousness.

c. He may become harsh.

3. If the restorer falls, then the needy person may say, "What right has he to speak to me; look what he does. I am not guilty of that."

## Comment 6:2

**Bear one another's burdens**

1. Christians must have strong shoulders.

2. Paul writes, "Love believeth all things, hopeth all things, endureth all things." I Cor. 13:7

3. Note how the early church did this.

a. "Them that believed were of one heart and soul." Acts 4:32-36

4. Sharing only goes so far — it has some limitation.

a. "If any will not work, neither let him eat." II Thess. 3:10

5. Consider the word *weight* or *burden*.

a. The word means an excessive weight, such as it is a toil to carry.

b. "Now we that are strong ought to bear the infirmities of the weak, and not to please ourselves." Rom. 15:1

## Comment 6:3

**fulfill the law of Christ**

1. What is the law of Christ?

a. "A new commandment I give unto you, that ye love one another." Jn. 13:34

b. "This is my commandment, that ye love one another." Jn. 15:12

**thinketh himself to be something**

1. This refers to those who think they are "big ones" when they are "zeros."

a. People, who if bought for their worth and sold at their evaluation, would net a great profit.

b. "If I have the gift of prophecy and know all mysteries and all knowledge; and if I have all faith, so as to remove mountains, but have not love, I am nothing." I Cor. 13:2

2. There are those who like to eulogize themselves.

3. These are puffed up to their own destruction.

a. "Love . . . is not puffed up." I Cor. 13:4

b. "Let no man rob you of your prize by a voluntary humility and worshipping of the angels, dwelling in the things which he hath seen, vainly puffed up by his fleshly mind." Col. 2:18

1) A spiritual mind will be humble.

2) Puffing up prepares for a bubble to burst.

c. "That in us ye might learn not to go beyond the things which are written; that no one of you be puffed up for the one against the other." I Cor. 4:6

d. "Now as concerning things sacrificed to idols: We know that we all have knowledge. Knowledge puffeth up, but love edifieth." I Cor. 8:1

1) Those who are Ph.D.'s in their thinking, but not in their training, often are trouble makers.

2) The ignorant man knows not that he does not know.

**he deceiveth himself.**
1. A magician can do strange things with others.
2. The puffed up person can strangely fool himself.
a. There is no one more miserable than the self-deluded person.
b. "If any man thinketh himself to be religious, while he bridleth not his tongue but deceiveth his heart, this man's religion is vain." James 1:26

## Comment 6:4

**But let a man prove his own works**
1. *Prove* means to examine.
a. See I Cor. 11:28. Let a man examine himself at the table.
b. Rom. 12:2
2. We have to give account of our own life, therefore we must be concerned. Cf. Rom. 2:6; 14:12; Gal. 6:8; II Cor. 5:10

**Then shall he have his glorying in regard of himself alone**
1. See II Cor. 1:12 for the meaning of this. "For our glorying is this, the testimony of our conscience, that in holiness and sincerity of God, not in fleshly wisdom but in the grace of God, . . ."
a. A thorough examination of self, leaves no room for self-glory.
b. The grace of God is our glory and it eliminates the big "I".
2. If a person is egotistical, he compares himself with what is inferior and thereby exhalts himself all the more.
a. Illustration—A robin saw itself in a mirror, ruffled up its feathers, and found itself destroying itself by its own image.
b. Such a person will hang himself, for he keeps giving himself enough rope.

**And not of his neighbor**
1. The Catholic Bible reads, "And not in comparison with another."
2. He will not have time to glory over his neighbor's weakness.
3. He will not be like the Pharisee: "God I thank thee that I am not as the rest of men." Luke 18:11

## Comment 6:5

**For each man shall bear his own burden**
1. This sounds like a contradiction of verse 2.
2. The Greek word means — burden or responsibility.
a. Jesus said, "My yoke is easy and my burden is light." Matt. 11:30

b. "For they bind heavy burdens and grievous to be borne and lay them on men's shoulders." Matt. 23:4

c. This word is different from "burden" of verse 2. Here it means toil, trials.

3. Each one of us shall bear his own load of duty and accountibility.

a. This we will be called upon to answer for in the judgment.

b. No one can shoulder our responsibility for us.

### Study Questions 6:1-5

884. With what word does Paul open this chapter?

885. May we assume that Paul was not yet ready to disfellowship them for their false teaching?

886. Define the word *overtaken*.

887. Explain the meaning of *trespass*.

888. What is the idea of a "besetting sin?"

889. Is this a sin committed by the will or against it?

890. Who were the spiritual ones?

891. Were they the most saintly ones?

892. Could it refer to the ones with spiritual gifts?

893. What is meant by the word *restore?*

894. How do you go about it?

895. Are there impossible ones? (Cf. Heb. 6:4-5)

896. What do you do if one refuses you? (Cf. Titus 3:10)

897. What kind of a spirit does the restoring one need?

898. What is meant by gentleness?

899. Why do you need to look to yourself?

900. Is it possible to forget your own weakness while looking at the weakness of others?

901. Is there any danger in trying to help people?

902. Is it possible for a person to be unlovely while speaking on the subject?

903. What would you look for in self while counseling?

904. Does the verse mean that you may fall into their temptations?

905. In what way is this a very real problem?

906. Define *fear*.

907. Are Christians to be burden bearers?

908. Did the early church set us an example?

909. Paul teaches that burden bearing does what?
910. Can we go to the extreme in slave-driving responsibilities?
911. What warning is given in this verse?
912. How do people get big ideas about themselves?
913. Is it possible for a person to be nothing?
914. What is the danger of being puffed up?
915. Does knowledge puff up people?
916. Do people become proud of their spirituality?
917. Can a person play the part of a magician?
918. How does one fool himself?
919. When a man examines his work, how should he compare it?
920. When we compare ourselves with others, what kind of a person do we select?
921. When we glorify ourselves in comparison to others, what do we generally do to the other individual?
922. Will we glory in self if we compare ourselves to Christ?
923. How often should we prove our work?
924. Do we have teaching encouraging self-examination once a week? Cf. I Cor. 11:28
925. Is this verse a contradiction of verse 2?
926. What does *burden* mean?
927. Did Jesus urge burden-bearing?
928. If we shoulder other people's burdens, should we expect others to shoulder ours?

2. Material support for the Gospel 6:6-10

## Text 6:6-8

**6 But let him that is taught in the word communicate unto him that teacheth in all good things. 7 Be not deceived; God is not mocked: for whatsoever a man soweth, that shall he also reap. 8 For he that soweth unto his own flesh shall of the flesh reap corruption; but he that soweth unto the Spirit shall of the Spirit reap eternal life.**

## Paraphrase

6 Now let him who is instructed in the doctrines and precepts of the gospel, impart a share of all the good things he enjoys to the instructor. By this good work, ye may have matter of boasting in yourselves, ver. 4.

7. To maintain them who teach you, is your duty. Therefore, do not deceive yourselves, God will not be mocked: For, as in the natural, so in the moral world, whatever a man soweth, that also he shall reap.

8 Therefore he who, by spending his time and wealth in gratifying his sensual desires, soweth into his own flesh, shall from such a sensual life reap corruption; the utter destruction of his soul and body. But he who, by spending his time and wealth in improving his mind, and in doing good to others, soweth into his spirit, shall, from such sowing into the spirit, assuredly reap life everlasting.

## Comment 6:6

### Let him that is taught in the word communicate

1. Let the one taught remunerate his teacher.
a. In financial aid.
1) "Even so did the Lord ordain that they that proclaim the gospel should live of the gospel." I Cor. 9:14
2) "I robbed other churches, taking wages of them that I might minister unto you." II Cor. 11:8
a. Some folk are against ministerial support.
1) Elder: "Preachers are to sacrifice, therefore I am against a raise in salary."
2) Lady: "Keep him humble Lord; we will do all we can to keep him poor."
b. In honor and reverance, and all other good things.
1) To talk ill of the preacher before your children is bad.
2) Talk ill of the preacher in the community — and it will help convince them of the hypocrisy of religion.
3) The teacher represents God and therefore should demand respect.
2. The student of the Word should learn to support the teacher of the Word.
Cf. I Tim. 5:17; II Cor. 9:7-8

## Comment 6:7

### Be not deceived

1. This suggests you can do something about being deceived.
a. Man is a thinking individual.
b. He is a willing individual.

2. How are men deceived?

a. They are deceived by the devil. "Satan . . . shall deceive the nations." Rev. 20:7-8

b. They are ensnared by the devil. "Moreover he must have good testimony from them that are without; lest he fall into reproach and the snare of the devil." I Tim. 3:7

1) "And they may recover themselves out of the snare of the devil, having been taken captive by him unto his will." II Tim. 2:26

c. The devil works lying wonders.

1) "With all power and signs and lying wonders, and with all deceit of unrighteousness." II Thess. 2:9

2) "Spirits of demons, working signs." Rev. 16:14

d. Satan assumes the form of an angel of light.

1) "Satan fashioneth himself into an angel of light." II Cor. 11:14

e. Satan blinds men: "The God of this world hath blinded the minds." II Cor. 4:4

f. Satan tempts men: "The tempter had tempted you." I Thess. 3:5

g. Man deceives himself.

1) "Each man is tempted, when he is drawn away by his own lust, and enticed." James 1:14

3. What can be done about it?

a. God knows how to deliver saints out of temptation.

1) II Peter 2:9

2) I Cor. 10:13

3) Heb. 2:18

b. Man can do something about it.

1) Man can resist in faith. Eph. 6:16 and I Pet. 5:9-10

2) Man can watch against it. I Pet. 5:8

3) Man can pray to be kept from it. Matt. 6:13; 26:41

**God is not mocked**

1. *Mocked* in the original verb meant to writhe the nostril — to scorn or sneer.

2. Man in false appearances only deceives himself.

a. Gehazi, the servant of Elisha, wanted to collect from Naaman for the healing of leprosy. II Kings 5:15-27

b. Ananias and Sapphira tried to deceive Peter. Acts 5:1-10
3. The mocking shall work in reverse.
a. "The kings of the earth set themselves against Jehovah." Psalms 2:4
1) Like man disturbing an ant hill, the ants go in confusion.
2) Man drinks, carouses, rejects Christ, builds empires — then floods, earthquakes, droughts, etc., come to take it all away.

**for whatsoever a man soweth**

1. A man can sow for the devil.
a. He can sow discord. Prov. 6:14, 19
b. He can sow strife. Prov. 16:28
c. He can sow iniquity. Prov. 22:8
d. He can sow to the flesh. Gal. 6:8
2. A man can sow for God.
a. "I planted, Apollos watered." I Cor. 3:6
b. "Soweth the word." Mark 4:14
c. "Seed to the sower." II Cor. 9:10 and Matt. 13:38

**that shall he also reap**

1. This is a certainty in life.
a. If he has sown for God, it will be bountiful.
1) "He that soweth sparingly shall reap also sparingly; and he that soweth bountifully shall reap also bountifully." II Cor. 9:6
2) "Open windows of heaven." Malachi 3:10
3) "He that supplieth seed to the sower and bread for food, shall supply and multiply your seed for sowing, and increase the fruits of your righteousness." II Cor. 9:10
4) "It is sown a natural body; it is raised a spiritual body. If there is a natural body, there is also a spiritual body." I Cor. 15:44
b. If he has sown for the devil, it will be frightful.
1) "For they sow the wind and they shall reap the whirlwind." Hosea 8:7
2) "They that . . . sow trouble, reap the same." Job 4:8
3) "Shall reap corruption." Gal. 6:8
2. We live in a dependable universe, therefore we are both blessed and warned.

## Comment 6:8

### reap corruption

1. The flesh is poor soil for a spiritual harvest.
a. It lusts against the spirit.
b. It is subject to death.
c. It is weakness.
2. Gratification of flesh alone will bring corruption.
a. The verbal noun suggests decay or the condition of being impaired, spoiled, wasted away. Col. 2:22; Rom. 8:21
b. It is used of corruption in our moral nature.
1) II Pet. 1:4
2) II Pet. 2:12-22
3) II Cor. 7:2
4) I Tim. 6:5
c. It is used of the rotting away of the dead body.
1) Acts 2:27
2) Acts 2:31
3) Acts 13:34-37
d. It is the antithesis of our inheritance.
1) "It is sown in corruption; it is raised in incorruption." I Cor. 15:42
2) "Neither doth corruption inherit incorruption." I Cor. 15:50

### shall reap eternal life

1. A new body will be fashioned for such people.
a. "It is raised a spiritual body." I Cor. 15:42-54
b. "Fashion anew the body of our humiliation, that it may be conformed to the body of his glory." Phil. 3:21
c. "If the earthly house of our tabernacle be dissolved, we have . . . a house not made with hands, eternal." II Cor. 5:1
d. "For as in Adam all die, even so in Christ shall all be made alive." I Cor. 15:22
2. New glory will be harvested.
a. Rom. 2:7
b. I Cor. 15:49
c. I Cor. 15:43
d. I Tim. 6:17-19
3. How do you sow to the Spirit?
a. By deeds to fellow men.

1) "Rich in good works, ready to distribute." I Tim. 6:17-18
2) The Rich young ruler failed in this. Lk. 18:22
3) Jesus said, "Ye have done it unto me." Matt. 25:45
b. By love for God
1) "Present your bodies a living sacrifice." Rom. 12:1-2
2) "Lay not up for yourselves." Matt. 6:19
3) "But seek ye first his kingdom." Matt. 6:33
c. By devotion to Jesus Christ.

### Study Questions 6:6-8

929. Who are the taught ones?
930. What is meant by "in the word?"
931. Does this refer to preachers, elders, and Bible School teachers?
932. Does the word *communicate* mean to hold conversation here?
933. What does it mean?
934. Does it mean good financial support?
935. Prove by the Scriptures that teachers and preachers are to be supported financially.
936. Did Paul receive financial help?
937. Was this always so?
938. What is included in the expression "all good things?"
939. Name some good things that a preacher or teacher might appreciate most.
940. Can man fool God?
941. Can man fool himself into thinking he can?
942. How are men deceived?
943. What methods does the devil use?
944. Does God do anything about our temptations?
945. How can man resist the devil's cunning?
946. What does the word *mock* mean?
947. What actually takes place when a man tries to mock God?
948. What is meant by *sowing?*
949. How does a man sow evil?
950. What kind of evil is it possible to sow?
951. Describe sowing good for God.
952. Does this verse speak uncertainly?
953. Is a harvest assured regardless of how we sow?
954. Who will supply us good seed to sow?

955. Is the flesh good or bad soil for sowing?
956. What will sowing to the flesh bring?
957. Define *corruption*.
958. Give verses that teach man's corruption.
959. Explain spiritual sowing.
960. When do we do spiritual planting?
961. Is there a second chance?
962. What is included in the spiritual reaping?
963. What will happen to the body that is buried, if we are spiritual?
964. What chapter in Corinthians is given over to the subject of the resurrection?

## Text 6:9, 10

**And let us not be weary in well doing: for in due season we we shall reap, if we faint not. 10 So then, as we have opportunity, let us work that which is good toward all men, and especially toward them that are of the household of the faith.**

### Paraphrase

9 Wherefore, having such a prospect, let us not flag in improving our minds, and in doing good to others: For in the proper season, namely at the judgment, we shall reap the blessed harvest of everylasting life, if we faint not.

10 Certainly, then, while the season of sowing lasteth, let us work good to all men, whatever their country or their religion may be, but especially to them who are of the family of God by faith: for, considering our persecuted state, we ought to be very attentive in succouring one another.

### Comment 6:9

**And let us not be wearing in well doing: for in due season we shall reap, if we faint not**

(This calls for a favorite sermon outline)

AN EXHORTATION TO THE PEOPLE OF GOD.

I. Be not weary — exhortation to not be tired — to keep on the job.
1. Tiredness is largely mental.
a. Children play without tiring.
1) Illustration: Man experimented: did everything the child did and he was soon exhausted.

2) Illustration: Put that child to work, and it soon is exhausted.

2. Church folks are sissies — too tired for worship.
a. Look at your night club people and the hours they keep. A church person couldn't (wouldn't) go to church like that.
b. Church people
1) Can't get up on Sunday Morning.
2) Can't come on Sunday evening.
3) You would think it took a rugged constitution to stand a twenty minute sermon.
4) It would seem by the excuses that only those who have nothing to do but recuperate for church could make it.

3. We are tired in soul winning.
a. Folk are so exhausted from work that they can't get out to win souls.
b. There are four or five tavern owners for every church in town, and the taverns thrive.

4. We are called to outwork the devil.

II. Exhortation to do good work — "In well doing."

1. This refers to spiritual work.
a. We have examples.
1) "Even Jesus of Nazareth, who went about doing good." Acts 10:38
2) "Dorcas, full of good works." Acts 9:36-39
3) The Apostles preached boldly.
4) "They that were scattered abroad went about preaching." Acts 8:4

b. We have a book that will show us what is "well doing."
1) "Furnished completely unto every good work." II Tim. 3:16-17
a. There is no need of the Book of Mormon.
b. Mrs. Eddy's book is superfluous.
c. The Bible does a complete job.

c. We are warned about failure to do good.
1) "To him therefore that knoweth to do good, and doeth it not, to him it is sin." James 4:17

2. Our good should be directed first to God's people. "Especially unto them of the household of faith." Gal. 6:10
a. We must have a loyalty to one another.

1) Christian folk gossip, back bite, speak unkindly.
2) Let us keep our skeletons in the closet.
3) Labor unions, lodges, etc., have a close fellowship, sometimes more than the church people.
4) We fail to do business with one another — spend money with heathen in preference to patronizing the Christian.
b. A faithfulness here will impress the world.
1) "Behold how good and how pleasant . . . for brethren to dwell together in unity". Psalm 133:1
2) "By this shall all men know that ye are my disciples, if ye have love one for another." John 13:35

III. Consider the time element — "we shall in due season."

1. Here is an exhortation to be patient.
a. We are too much like children who want everything now.
1) On a trip they want to arrive at once.
2) Time means little to little children.
b. Folk want to save everybody in a short revival but give up quickly when only a few respond.
c. A few invitations and they give up and say "I told you so: people are not interested in revival today."

2. A righteous cause in dealing with people needs time to work out.
a. Evil is deeply entrenched.
b. Prejudices are not easily broken down.
c. Most folk quit after a few failures — that is what the devil wants.

3. Remember — God works on time.
a. "When the fulness of time came." Gal. 4:4

IV. A certainty — "We shall reap."

1. God will see to it that there will be a reaping.
a. "I planted — Apollos watered, but God gave the increase." I Cor. 3:6
b. "We shall reap" rings with faith and victory. Gal. 6:9
c. "My word . . . It shall not return unto me void." Isaiah 55:11

2. This makes a dependable universe.
a. We never waste time when we work for God — nor is it in vain.

b. God is as dependable in the spiritual realm as He is in the physical.

V. A provision that is conditional — "If we faint not."

1. We can't quit like spoiled children.
a. Children say, "I'll take my dolly and go home."
b. Children work a while then quit — can't work long.
2. Jesus urged toil and steadfastness on His disciples.
a. "In your patience ye shall win your souls." Luke 21:19
b. "Be thou faithful." Rev. 2:10
c. "He that endureth to the end." Matt. 10:22
d. ". . . having put his hand to the plow . . ." Luke 9:62
3. This is a cruel hard universe — the devil will defeat you in the heat of the day unless you take God seriously.
a. "I can do all things in him." Phil. 4:13
b. "No temptation but such as man can bear." I Cor. 10:13

## Comment 6:10

### as we have therefore opportunity

1. The alert Christian sees opportunity everywhere.
2. Serious-minded people know that good work is urgent. Cf. John 9:4
a. Death takes away opportunities.
b. We pass this way once and once only and opportunities are lost forever.

### Let us do good unto all men

1. Our good should be directed first toward those of God.

2. All men are our brothers — neighbors.
a. The story of the good Samaritan makes this evident. Lk. 10:33
b. Doing good is proof of our love, said John.
"Hereby know we love, because he laid down his life for us: and we ought to lay down our lives for the brethren. But whoso hath the world's goods, and beholdeth his brother in need, and shutteth up his compassion from him, how doth the love of God abide in him?" I Jn. 3:16-17

3. A summary of Jesus life in that "He went about doing good." Acts 10:38
a. Most of us go about more than Jesus but there is very little good attached.

b. Dorcas is a good example of good deeds who certainly followed the Lord's example.

### Especially to them of the household of faith

1. Let it be said of us, "How they love one another."
2. The members of the same body must care for one another.
3. The members of the same household should manifest love for the children of God.
4. It is good to do business with the household of faith rather than to prefer the bargains of the heathen.

## Study Questions 6:9, 10

965. Is weariness something that we can control?
966. Does your life speak of a spiritual tiredness?
967. Does the world exhibit more energy for its sowing than does the Church?
968. Are we tired in soul winning before the revival is over?
969. What is meant by *well doing*?
970. Was Jesus a good example?
971. How about Dorcas?
972. Is the Bible a sufficient guide in well doing?
973. Are we doing good when we bite and devour one another?
974. Is a time limit involved here?
975. How do we know when the due season is up?
976. Who is the time keeper?
977. Do we have a right to place a time limit on the germination of spiritual seed?
978. Does God work on time? Cf. Gal. 4:4
979. Paul says "we shall reap." Is this to mean certainty?
980. Who will see to it that a harvest will come?
981. What if this were not a dependable universe at all?
982. What condition does God put on our harvest?
983. Define *faint not*.
984. What kind of people grow weary?
985. Give scriptures that urge faithfulness, steadfastness, etc.
986. Who will win if we faint?
987. Do you think that the devil is present in the heat of the harvest to cause you to faint?
988. Does this verse suggest that we have opportunity, or that we have to make it?

989. To whom should good work be directed?
990. Who should especially receive our goodness?
991. Does the good Samaritan story fit here? Compare I John 3:16-17 in regard to good work.
992. Who is included in the household of faith?

## D. CONCLUSION

1. Token of Authorship. (Cf. II Thess. 3:17) 6:11

### Text 6:11-13

**11 See with how large letters I write unto you with mine own hand. 12 As many as desire to make a fair show in the flesh, they compel you to be circumcised; only that they may not be persecuted for the cross of Christ. 13 For not even they who receive circumcision do themselves keep the law; but they desire to have you circumcised, that they may glory in your flesh.**

### Paraphrase

11 Ye see how large a letter I have written to you with my own hand. By this ye may understand my anxiety to preserve you in the true faith of the gospel.

12 As many of your teachers as wish to appear fair in the eyes of their unbelieving brethren, by their attachment to the law, these strongly persuade you to be circumcised, not because they think circumcision necessary to salvation, but only that they may not be persecuted by the unbelieving Jews, for preaching salvation through a crucified Messiah.

13 These hypocrites do not enjoin circumcision on any conscientious motives; for not even do the circumcised themselves keep the law of Moses; but they wish you to be circumcised, merely that they may boast, among the unbelieving Jews, of having persuaded you to receive that rite in your flesh.

### Comment 6:11

**See with how large letters I write unto you with mine own hand**

1. The closing words written in his own hand-writing would prove its authorship.
2. Some think *large* refers to the length and not the size of the letters.

2. The motives of the Judaisers compared with that of the Apostles. 6:12-16

## Comment 6:12

**As many as desire to make a fair show**

1. Jewish religion carried some respectability.
2. It didn't demand very much — Christianity was so strict.
3. If they had presented the Cross with its simplicity, they would have offended their unbelieving countrymen.

**Only that they may not be persecuted for the cross of Christ**

1. Catholic Bible: "That they may not suffer persecution for the Cross."
2. It would be a temptation to the weak Christian to swing over to Judaism to escape the persecution.
3. This would make him credited among his brethren.

## Comment: 6:13

**For neither they who are circumcised keep the law**

1. They professed Judaism — not from a desire to conform to the will of God but because Judaism was popular.
2. These are the kind of teachers you have ,they do not keep the law — all of it.

**But desire to have you circumcised that they may glory in your flesh**

1. It is not for the sake of their righteousness, although that impression is given.
2. They force it on them that they may glory in their submission.
3. The false teachers persuaded them from insincere motives.

## Study Questions 6:11-13

993. Did Paul make a mistake when he spoke of *largeness* in verse 11 and then wrote a small letter to the Galatians?
994. Did it refer to the length of the letter or the size of his handwriting?
995. Why did Paul want them to see his own handwriting?
996. What is meant by fair show?
997. Was early Christianity interested in respectability as are the major denominations today?
998. What would a fleshly show refer to?
999. What is meant by *constrain?*
1000. Would weak Christians give over to a false teaching to avoid persecution or pressure?
1001. Were those who demanded circumcision faithful to all the law?
1002. Were the "show-offs" persuaded that circumcision was essential for salvation?

1003. What accusation does Paul make here?
1004. Why would they want some to keep part of it when they were not enthusiastic enough to keep all of it?
1005. How would their trouble-makers glory in the flesh of their proselytes?
1006. Could it mean that they would glory in their submission?
1007. If we submit to false teaching with sincere motives, does that make it right?

## Text 6:14-16

**14 But far be it from me to glory, save in the cross of our Lord Jesus Christ, through which the world hath been crucified unto me, and I unto the world. 15 For neither is circumcision anything, nor uncircumcision, but a new creature. 16 And as many as shall walk by this rule, peace be upon them, and mercy, and upon the Israel of God.**

## Paraphrase

14 But let it never happen to me to boast, except in salvation through the cross of our Lord Jesus Christ, by which the world is crucified to me—is rendered incapable, either of alluring me by its pleasures, or of terrifying me by its frowns—and I am crucified to the world: I am rendered incapable of its sinful practices, and sinful pleasures.

15 I boast in the cross of Christ, as the only foundation of my hope of salvation, and as the great principle of my sanctification: Because, under the gospel, neither circumcision nor uncircumcision is of any avail towards our acceptance with God, but the being a new creature.

16 Now as many of the believing Gentiles as walk by this rule, seeking acceptance with God, not by circumcision, but by becoming new creatures, may peace be their portion in this life, and pardon at the day of judgment. The same blessing I wish on the believing Jews.

## Comment 6:14

**far be it from me to**
1. Paul had much right to glory
a. Glory in his noble fleshly birth. Phil. 3:4-5; II Cor. 11:18
b. Glory in his religious attainments. Phil. 3:4-5
c. Glory in his zeal. Phil. 3:6

1) Few men travelled farther to preach.
2) Few had had more converts.
3) Few had established more churches.
d. Cf. Rom. 15:17, I Cor. 9:16, II Cor. 5:12, II Cor. 12:1-9.
2. God deserves all the glory when His children accomplish something worthwhile.
a. A Christian can do great things for God if he does not worry about who gets the credit.
b. God gives the increase to seed sown faithfully.
3. Evidently some gloried in their wicked ways among the Galatians, even against the cross.

### save in the cross of our Lord

1. Glory in the salvation that is found in the cross, not circumcision.
2. We can rejoice that we are permitted to suffer for it.
a. "Blessed are ye." Matt. 5:11-12
b. "We also rejoice in our tribulations." Rom. 5:3

### through which the world hath been crucified unto me

1. The world is dead to Paul—no life—no attraction.
2. He could condemn the world.
3. Monks in monasteries believed that they were crucifying the world unto themselves, but the monasteries became dens of iniquity.

### And I unto the world

1. The world condemns him.
2. Paul could say "I detest the world" — but it detests us.
3. We despise the world—but it despises us also.

## Comment 6:15

### but a new creature

1. New birth is the important thing.
2. The new man counts; circumcision is not in it.
3. Some characteristics of the new creation are:
a. A new spirit.
b. A new will.
c. A new attitude.
4. Cf. Col. 3:10; Gal. 3:27

## Comment 6:16

### As many as shall walk by this rule

1. *This rule* — refers to the teaching concerning the new creation.
2. Man is saved by the cross of Jesus — not circumcision.

### peace be upon them, and mercy

1. Such people as abide by this, enjoy the peace, favor, and forgiveness of God.
2. These are fruit of the Spirit and Paul desires these for them.

### upon the Israel of God

1. The true Christians are the Israel of God — as distinguished from the Israel according to the flesh.
a. Rom. 2:29
b. Rom. 4:12

2. Obedience to Christ made them a part of the true Israel. Cf. Phil. 3:3; Col. 2:11; Rom. 3:29-30

## Study Questions 6:14-16

1008. What does Paul mean by *far be it from me?*
1009. Define *glory.*
1010. In what realm did Paul feel that he could glory?
1011. How could one glory in the cross?
1012. Should we glory in the privilege of salvation?
1013. Would this exalt us or humble us?
1014. Paul has taught the crucifixion of himself. Does he mean that the world is crucified too?
1015. Does he mean that the world is dead as far as attractiveness to him is concerned?
1016. What does he mean "I unto the world?"
1017. Does the world in its pleasure want the Christian dead to it?
1019. Through what was the world crucified unto Paul?
1019. Is verse 15 like a previous verse?
1020. Who makes ritual of no consequence?
1021. What does it mean to be in Christ?
1022. How do we become new creatures?
1023. Is circumcision in this process, according to Paul in this verse?
1024. What really counts?
1025. What rule is referred to here?
1026. How inclusive is *as many?*

1027. Is Paul pronouncing "peace" or teaching that new creatures will have it?
1028. Define *mercy*.
1029. Whose mercy are they to have—Paul's or God's?
1030. Who are the Israel of God?
1031. Does this mean fleshly Israel or spiritual Israel?
1032. Are you then an Israelite?

3. A refutation of the charges by the Judaisers. 6:17

## Text 6:17-18

**17 Henceforth let no man trouble me; for I bear branded on my body the marks of Jesus. 18 The grace of our Lord Jesus Christ be with your spirit, brethren. Amen.**

## Paraphrase

17 Henceforth, let no one give me trouble, by calling my commission, my doctrine, or my faithfulness in question: For I bear the marks of the Lord Jesus's servant in my body.

18 May the love of our Lord Jesus Christ be alway felt in your mind, brethren. Amen.

## Comment 6:17

### Henceforth let no man trouble me
1. "Let no man give me trouble." (Catholic Bible)
2. Put an end to your troubles — your contentions. Turn back to the pure doctrine and all will be well.
3. Church trouble is the kind that Christians ought not to have.

### I bear branded on my body the marks of Jesus
1. One who has suffered for Jesus like Paul, can see only foolishness in the mark of circumcision.
2. This probably refers to marks on his body from persecution.
a. "God hath set forth us the apostles last of all, as men doomed to death: for we are made a spectacle unto the world, both to angels and men." I Cor. 4:9
b. "In stripes . . . in deaths . . . beaten . . . stoned." II Cor. 11:23-25

4. Benediction  6:18

## Comment 6:18

### Brethren
1. This is a contrast to "Foolish Galatians."
2. Paul felt the letter would make brethren of them.

196

**The grace of our Lord Jesus Christ be with your spirit**

1. The grace of God can only work with the spirit of man.
2. This is his benediction upon them.
3. If their spirit would work in harmony with the grace of God, they could be restored to grace.

**Unto the Galatians written from Rome** (King James)

1. This part does not appear in the best manuscripts.
2. The Syriac says, "The end of the epistle to the Galatians which was written from Rome."
3. The Ethiopic says, "To the Galatians."
4. The Vulgate says nothing additional.
5. The Arabic says, "Written from the city of Rome by Titus and Luke."

## Study Questions 6:17, 18

1033. Does this verse infer that the false teachers had bothered Paul?
1034. Does it mean that his erring brethren were bothering him?
1035. Is this an exhortation to follow truth or suggesting to them to let him forget them?
1036. Is he comparing his sufferings, beatings, stripes, etc., to shame them for submitting to circumcision?
1037. What are the marks of Jesus upon him?
1038. Did anyone use a branding iron on him?
1039. Does Paul claim them as Christians even though they have fallen from grace?
1040. Is it possible that he counted on the letter to restore them, so that by the time they had read this far, they would be brethren again?
1041. Are the final words considered a benediction?
1042. How could he wish grace upon them, when he has accused them of being out of it?
1043. If Paul believed in the power of the word, could he not believe that this divine epistle would restore them?
1044. What did he mean *with your spirit?*

## Questions on Galatians, Chapter Six

### Choice:

1. If a man be overtaken in any trespass
    1. excommunicate him
    2. let him alone so he can conquer it
    3. restore such a one in gentleness

2. Bear ye one anothers burdens
    1. so yours will be lighter
    2. so fulfill the law of Christ
    3. so the person will not be overpowered

3. Whatsoever a man soweth
    1. that shall he also reap
    2. the same will sprout
    3. will blossom in the spring
    4. will have to go fight weeds

4. Let us not be weary
    1. in well doing
    2. because you can't work if tired
    3. because the apostles were not wearied

5. We should do good to those of the household of faith
    1. when we're in the mood
    2. providing we shall receive good from him
    3. when we have opportunity

6. Paul gloried
    1. in the Cross of Christ
    2. in his great popularity
    3. in the fact that he had learned to write at the feet of Gamaliel

7. At the close of the epistle Paul pleads with them to give him
    1. a great offering from the heart
    2. no more trouble
    3. acceptance of the law

8. In the latter part of Galatians Paul is speaking
    1. more kindly
    2. more doctrinally
    3. more sternly

9. The result of sowing spiritual things is
    1. a trouble free life
    2. many friends
    3. life everlasting

10. Paul said,
    1. he bore in his body the marks of Jesus
    2. the Galatians would be overcome by the Romans
    3. he could preach superior to others

11. The one that is taught in the word should
    1. listen carefully
    2. take notes
    3. communicate unto him that teacheth

12. Paul speaks concerning his hand writing—
    1. he was left handed
    2. he apologized for poor writing
    3. he wrote with large letters

13. Paul says we shall reap in due season
    1. if we live that long
    2. if we faint not
    3. if we sowed good seed

14. The good that we do should be directed
    1. to bring in the best returns
    2. in order to hit the target
    3. especially to the household of faith

15. This chapter is
    1. primarily doctrinal
    2. somewhat in the line of exhortation
    3. almost identical to the first

Coins used in Galatia in Paul's day and shortly thereafter.

## PISIDIAN ANTIOCH    ICONIUM

1

2

*(1) God of Antioch, MEN, with Phrygian cap. Long scepter in right hand and statue of cock at right foot; bull's head under left foot*

*(2) Zeus of Iconium, with scepter and thunderbolt. Coin of first century B.C.*

5

6

*(5) Cybele seated, with lions at her feet, wearing crown of towers and holding a tympanum. Coin of Gordian III, A.D. 224-244.*

*(6) Perseus destroying the opponents of Hellenism by holding up the head of Medusa. Coin of Hadrian, A.D. 117-138*